Forbidden Magic Spells From The Bible

Ancient Spells, Charms and Enchantments

Using Verses From the Old and New Testament

By Jessica C. Springfield

ZONTAR PUBLICATIONS

Forbidden Magic Spells From The Bible
Ancient Spells, Charms and Enchantments
Using Verses From The Old and New Testament

Jessica C. Springfield

First Printing

ISBN-13: 978-0692722978

ISBN-10: 0692722971

zontarpress@zoho.com

Contents

Forbidden Magic Spells From The Bible

FORWARD

THE IDEA behind Forbidden Magic Spells From The Bible is simple; all verses in the Bible are charged with spiritual energies. This power of creation is called "LOGOS," meaning "WORD." It is thought that God the Creator used the LOGOS to initiate creation. The Universe and everything within it are divine words that have solidified. You can imagine that they were once dissolved in the sound vibrations of the divine cosmic word. Each thing we see is a divine word become solid.

In this way we can understand the deeper meaning of the beginning of *The Gospel According to John*:

> "In the beginning was the Word,
> and the Word was with God,
> and a God was the Word.
>
> The Word was with God at the beginning,
> and through it all things came to be;
> no single thing was created without it."

Everything that came into existence emerged from the Word.

According to Rudolf Steiner, when we take these statements as literally as possible, it is easy to acknowledge the creative power of the Word or logos. LOGOS must not be translated as anything except word, because this passage means that the unspoken creative word underlies all external creation. The resounding word is the source of everything that exists. If we went back through the ages, we would hear all the objects and beings we now know as animals, plants, minerals, and humans resounding through cosmic space.

For centuries, people have been using the Holy Scripture to induce magical principles. Some of this has come down to us in the magical practices of Hoodoo and Folk magic.

Forbidden Magic Spells From The Bible

The majority of these ancient techniques have been handed down from generation to generation strictly by word of mouth and little has actually ever been written down. Because of this, the secret of Bible magic has been kept within small groups scattered across the globe. Many have no idea that other practitioners of the ancient art even exist. The rise of evangelical Christianity has forced many Bible magic adepts to go underground, or even give up practicing altogether.

For a long time churches have taught that all magic is inherently evil and that anyone who practices it is to be condemned and possibly even put to death. This has little actually to do with a few verses in the Bible that speak against witches and diviners, and more to do with the churches power base that has held control over the people for centuries.

It is our divine right as children of Creation to understand and glorify the secrets of the Universe. God, the Creative force of reality has provided for us the powers of creation, handed down from the Eons in the form of words that resonate with the energies of Creation. Despite what the ministers, priests and imams have tried to suppress, the power of Creation is within all of us, and it is Gods will that we use these powers to comprehend and eventually rejoice with Him the ultimate beauty of Creation.

I have spent years tracking down and interviewing practitioners of Bible magic in order to compile this book. While some have refused my requests, others are eager to share their knowledge with the rest of the world. Possibly for the first time ever, this ancient knowledge has been brought together in one comprehensive book.

The key to understanding Forbidden Magic Spells From The Bible is to realize that every word, every verse in the Holy Scriptures can be used for magic spells. Another point is the use of the word "Forbidden" in the title... forbidden, in this context, means that those ancient priests and Church Fathers who used these spells, meant to keep them secret but for a select few. Those who dared leak these ancient spells were put to death to insure that the "unwashed masses" could never realize the great power held by the elites. The techniques that I have compiled in this book are tried and true and have been used for centuries. However, once you understand the power behind these words, you are free to try your own spells using different verses not only from the Bible, but also from other Holy writings that were excluded from the Bible, other religious and spiritual writings, as well as inspirational writings and even poems.

Forbidden Magic Spells From The Bible

I. The Age of Magic

AT ONE time, the world was filled with magic. Ancient man saw magic in every aspect of his daily life. Everything was infused with sacred significance. The rising of the sun and moon, the wind that brings the rain, every rock, tree, river and mountain was imbued with spirit.

In those early days, religion and magic were inseparable. Magic was the way that man could interact with the gods and try to control an uncontrollable universe. The origins of magic were derived from necessity and desire; the necessity to live another day and the desire to better understand the mysteries of the world.

Today, magic is generally condemned by most major religions. The King James Version of the Bible has the famous translation "Thou shalt not suffer a witch to live" (Exodus 22:18), and Saul is rebuked by God for seeking advice from a diviner who could contact spirits. In the New Testament and later theology, it is thought that all seeming "magic" is actually powered by demons, making it even more unacceptable. Thus, magic was seen as taboo throughout much of the Middle Ages.

Modern Abrahamic theology claims that the age of miracles has passed, and "magic" is now ineffective. Because of this, it is unnecessary to hunt down witches, because there are no longer any true ones. Judaism has mostly lost its taste for killing magicians. The Jewish people have depended on tolerance of their host societies, and suggesting that undesirable people be driven away could upset the balance and end in their own persecution.

Evangelical Christians, however, still see the practice of magic and New Age philosophies as the work of the devil and demons. Many churches advocate a return to the "old ways" of stoning or burning anyone who practices magic.

11

Forbidden Magic Spells From The Bible

Of course this definition could include anything and everything that a church deems unchristian, including teaching evolution or reading Harry Potter books.

Many so-called "good Christians" would be horrified to know that many common Christian rituals would be considered magic by their broad definitions. In fact, the Bible has been used for magical purposes for centuries by people who would never consider themselves as practitioners of magic. Others, however, have fully realized that Forbidden Magic Spells From The Bible fits within the constraints of "sorcery" and have kept the truth to themselves, only allowing immediate family to learn the age-old practice.

Using the Bible for magical purposes is loosely known today as hoodoo, conjuring, granny, or folk magic. The practice can be simple or highly complicated and involves the recital of Psalms and selected Biblical verses for magical purposes according to Jewish and Christian magical traditions.

One source of inspiration came from Johannes Gottfried Seelig, who, according to Eoghan Ballard of the University of Pennsylvania, came to America from the Palatinate of Germany on June 12, 1694. Seeling was a follower of Johannes Kelpius, the leader of an often misunderstood band of millenarian pietists who were variously called "The Monks of the Wissahickon" or "The Woman in the Wilderness."

Their practice was fairly esoteric and they relied on astrology, were avid astronomers, and created the first recorded botanical garden in North America on a site occupied today by the Wissahickon Golf Course.

In 1720, Johann Conrad Beisell, the Eckerling brothers, Michael Wohlforth, Simon Koenig, Johan George Stiefel, Jacob Stuntz, and Isaac Van Bebber emigrated to Pennsylvania with the intent of joining Kelpius' group on the Wissahickon. Kelpius was by this time dead, leaving only an aging Matthaue and Seelig of the original community remaining faithful and still living in the hermitage. This was the first in a chain of events that led to the revival of esoteric Theosophy and Rosicrucian mysticism in Pennsylvania.

Beissel went on to found the much better known and understood monastic community in Ephrata, Pennsylvania, while the man he apprenticed himself to on the advice of Seelig and Matthaue, Peter Becker, founded the Dunkers, another Pennsylvania German religious community important in Moravian history.

The legend of "The Monks of the Wissahickon" grew more fantastic over the years as German ceased to be the language of the community in

Forbidden Magic Spells From The Bible

Germantown, the settlement nearest the Wissahickon, which was eventually incorporated into Philadelphia in the last century. So farfetched had the legends become, that one recent scholar actually claimed that this group practiced an early form of "neopaganism." Actually, they were well within the rubric of German Enlightenment esoteric Christianity and would have blanched to be called "pagan."

Interestingly, a tradition, probably an echo of an earlier tale told concerning Magister Kelpius, attached itself to the death of Johannes Gottfried Seelig, his follower. In this version of the death story, Seelig indicated a desire to William Levering to have his staff thrown into the nearby Schuylkill River. Upon its hitting the water it was reported to have exploded with a loud noise.

Seelig wrote a book called: *Secrets of the Psalms* that was first published in Germantown shortly after his death. Several editions from the 1700s and early 1800s in both German and English may be found in Philadelphia area museums and libraries.

In *Secrets of the Psalms*, Selig's general theme is that of the power of "names," a mystical Jewish Kabbalist belief that by properly pronouncing and invoking certain names of God, of angels, and of demons, one's wishes will be executed. This notion is conjoined with a medieval tradition that holds that many of the Psalms, particularly those attributed to King David, contain within them "seed sounds" or hidden syllables which, when spoken aloud, will cause magical works to be accomplished. The important Medieval Jewish book "Shimmush Tehillim" ("On the Use of Psalms") probably formed the basis for his work, and explains why *Secrets if the Psalms* was subtitled A Fragment of the Practical Kabala.

Kabbalah appeared in Jewish mystic circles in Spain and Southern France in the 12th century. Its oldest part, the Sefer Jetsira, was written between the third and sixth century. According to this belief God gave a second revelation to Moses together with the Law. It explained the secret meaning of the Law. This revelation is said to have been passed on down the ages by initiates. Kabbalistic studies in the Hebrew Scriptures developed in a theosophical mystique and sometimes in a sort of unintended religious magic.

Godfrey Selig considered himself a mystical Christian and felt it was God's wish that he compile the Hebrew source material and translate it into German. Selig was certain that Christians would embrace the material and accept it as part of God's ultimate plan for the church. Christian Kabbalists have been around since the 12th century, and Selig himself declared in his introduction that "the greatest and most genuine Kabbalists of the Jewish nation were nearly all followers and disciples of the blessed Saviour of the world."

Among the many results that proper recitation of the specific Psalms will produce, according to Selig's sources, are release from prison, safe childbirth, business success, safe travel, help in court cases, removal of enemies, and overcoming evil. Some of the Psalms are embellished with special prayers to be recited, actions to be performed, or holy names to be called upon.

The formula for the construction of the holy names involves an esoteric Kabbalistic letter-substitution method called "gematria" which Selig alludes to but does not fully explain. Some examples from Selig's book include:

Psalms for Making Peace between Husband and Wife -

Psalms 45 and 46 – Whoever has a scolding wife, let him pronounce the 45th Psalm over pure olive oil, and anoint his body with it, when his wife, in the future will be more lovable and friendly. But if a man has innocently incurred the enmity of his wife, and desires a proper return of conjugal love and peace, let him pray the 46th Psalm over olive oil, and anoint his wife thoroughly with it, and, it is said, married love will again return.

Psalm to Make Your Home Lucky -

Psalm 61 – When you are about to take possession of a new dwelling, repeat this Psalm just before moving in, with a suitable prayer, trusting in the name of Schaddei, and you will experience blessing and good fortune.

Psalm for Safe Travel at Night -

Psalm 121 – Are you compelled to travel alone by night, pray this Psalm reverently seven times, and you will be safe from all accidents and evil occurrences.

Forbidden Magic Spells From The Bible

Psalm for Severe Headache or Backache -

Psalm 3 – Whosoever is subject to severe headache and backache, let him pray this Psalm over a small quantity of olive oil, and anoint the head or back while in prayer. This will afford immediate relief.

Psalm for a Repentant Liar -

Psalm 132 – If you have sworn to perform anything punctually, and notwithstanding your oath you neglect to perform your obligation, and in this manner have perjured yourself, you should, in order to avoid a future crime of a similar kind, pray this Psalm daily with profound reverence.

Secrets of the Psalms is an artifact of the mystical Jewish belief in the magical efficacy of the recitation of God's Holy Word. That this tradition was mined by a millenarian Christian German and brought to America where it became a magical receipt-book, especially in the south and rural areas, is a good example of just one type of Bible magic that is still being practiced in secret all across the globe.

MYSTERY SCHOOLS

Christian magical practices are directly descended from the Mystery schools that were prevalent in ancient Egypt and Greece. In general, the classical philosophers looked down on magic and its practitioners. But the popular Greco-Egyptian philosophy of the Hermetic corpus contains magical elements even after purging by the Byzantine tradents, and the later Neoplatonists, such as Plotinus, renamed their magical practices "theurgy" and distinguished them from common magic.

The ancient philosophers believed that no man could live intelligently who did not have a fundamental knowledge of Nature and her laws. Before man can obey, he must understand. Our Western word Mystery comes from the Greek Musterion, meaning "secret thing." Its verb form mueo means "to initiate into the Mysteries," also "to instruct," and this in turn comes from muo, "to be shut or closed."

The term Mysteries signifies not only the plural of "mystery," but refers more specifically to the esoteric or mystical tradition of divine wisdom handed down from ancient times. As well, it refers to a wide variety of secret schools that existed prior to the Christian era throughout the Mediterranean and Near East.

Scholars call them the Mystery religions, and they are secretly connected to modern spiritual, mystical and even Judaism and Christian teaching. For example, there were the Eleusinian, Samothracian, Orphic, and Dionysian Mysteries in Greece, the Egyptian Mysteries of Isis and Osiris, and the Mithraic Mysteries of the Roman Empire. In ancient Greece the Mysteries were the secret heart of its religion, just as they were in other cultures from Ireland to Egypt to Mesopotamia and beyond.

The Mystery Schools were devoted to instructing man about the operation of divine law in the physical world. Few of the early schools actually worshiped manlike deities, although their symbolism might lead one to believe that they did. They taught man to use his faculties more intelligently, to be patient in the face of adversity, to be courageous when confronted by danger, to be true in the midst of temptation, and, most of all, to view a worthy life as the most acceptable sacrifice to God, and his body as an altar sacred to the Deity.

The antiquity of the Mystery tradition is documented in our oldest written records; and its teaching may be discerned in the spiritual expressions of peoples on every continent. In the prologue to the Gilgamesh Epic, for example, we find that Gilgamesh "was the one who saw the Great Deep. He was wise and knew everything; Gilgamesh, who saw secret things, opened the hidden place(s) and carried back a tale of the time before the Flood – he traveled the road, he was weary, worn out with labor, and, returning, engraved his story on stone." Looking at the secret meaning of that story, it is clear that it is an initiatory tale about the mysteries of death and rebirth, and about who and what we are as human beings.

While most of the inner rites and doctrines of the Mystery Schools have remained secret, their fundamental aim was never a mystery: the enlightenment and spiritual regeneration of humanity. Nor has the tradition's basic teachings, the divine source within, the universal brotherhood of life, altruism, and the inherent respect, consideration, and truthfulness due all beings, has ever been held back from public knowledge.

It is also taught that we as self-aware humans are fully and individually responsible for our thoughts and actions, both in our physical body and after its death; that our real being is "life" and that we are therefore the immortal craftsmen of our own destiny through the eternities.

We reap what we sow, no god or priest, savior or master can alter that. A true Mystery school is a spiritual system that can take an individual, wherever he/she is in present through all of the steps to enlightenment and ascension.

The word mystery does not mean elitism or secrecy. It means that the higher teachings and initiations are not revealed until the individual is properly prepared. It also means that the final stages of every path are truly a mystery that only the seeker can discover for himself, once the preparations have been completed. In other words, the final stage of awakening on everyone's path comes through self-discovery.

LOST WORLDS OF ANTIQUITY

Most of the Greek and Egyptian Mystery schools believed that their teachings were handed down from one or more ancient civilizations that were lost in antiquity. The Egyptian, Greek and Eleusinian schools especially taught that their secret knowledge had been brought to them by priests who had escaped from Atlantis before it was destroyed; others referred to the land of Hyperborea as the source of their great knowledge.

In ancient Egypt, Hermetism was the religion of the philosophical elite. In the ancient days, every nation had two religions. The first of these two was that of the philosophical elite which celebrated a pantheistic religion hidden among its Mystery schools. Second was the common religion which took the teachings of the Mystery schools and turned them into allegorical stories, or myths of gods and goddesses, themselves personifications of aspects of the Universe. The common man was seen as not having enough intelligence to comprehend the mysteries, and so took literally the polytheistic teachings.

In the case of Hermetism, Egyptian mythology was used in ceremonies practiced by the mystery schools at certain times of the year and initiations of members into various grades of access to their knowledge. It is said that both Plato and Moses was initiated into the Egyptian mystery schools in one of the subterranean halls of the Great Pyramid of Giza.

Using the mysteries taught by the Atlantean priests, Egyptian mystics could levitate, handle fire, live under water, sustain great pressure, harmlessly suffer mutilation, read the past, foretell the future, make themselves invisible, and cure disease. According to the historian Proclus, the initiated priests so fully understood the mutual sympathy between the visible and invisible worlds that they were able to change the course of action and focus divine virtues upon inferior natures.

The Egyptian priests taught that the visible and the invisible, or the seen and unseen, together constitute nature. Nature is as much an invisible world as it is a visible world. They recognized that the divine plan which underlies the world of Time, Space, and Causation cannot be accessed in the Macrocosm, but is available in the Microcosm, which was an internalization of faculties.

The ancient Egyptians believed that in remote antiquity gods had been with men; that deities and divine powers had walked the earth. This may be regarded as symbolical, however, it could be that in remote times humans were naturally mystical, possessing powers of extra sensory perception, and could communicate, understand, estimate, and react to the Divine principles upon which the universe is based.

Perhaps in those days the gods did walk among men, teaching them the divine secrets so that those who are ready to learn the Mysteries could also one day be taught. This is the principal of the Mystery schools, teaching the ultimate truth for those who are ready to learn it.

<u>CHRISTIANITY AND THE MYSTERY SCHOOLS</u>

Though modern Christians would be shocked to learn of their religions ancient connections with the Mystery schools; Christianity would not be as it is today without the teachings of the Mysteries. Most Christians do not realize that the terms mystery and mysteries are frequently used in the New Testament and carry the full sense of their original meaning of secret thing or teaching, including mystical knowledge about God, rebirth, and the afterlife. For example, Paul writes in his first letter to the Corinthians:

But we speak the wisdom of God in a mystery, even the hidden wisdom, which God ordained before the world unto our glory. – 2:7

And though I have the gift of prophecy, and understand all mysteries, and all knowledge; and though I have all faith, so that I could remove mountains, and have not love, I am nothing. – 13:2

Forbidden Magic Spells From The Bible

Behold, I show you a mystery; we shall not all sleep, but we shall all be changed . .
. the dead shall be raised incorruptible . . . and this mortal must put on immortality.

– 15:51-3

At a more fundamental level, each of the three synoptic gospels, Matthew, Mark, and Luke, uses the terms to emphasize the age-old pattern of esotericism, of inner teachings reserved for disciples in contrast to exoteric stories for the public.

Matthew 13:10-13 gives perhaps the fullest expression, revealing the purpose of parable, yet hiding it with paradox:

And the disciples came, and said unto him, Why speakest thou unto them in parables? He answered and said unto them, because it is given unto you to know the mysteries of the kingdom of heaven, but to them it is not given. Therefore speak I to them in parables: because they seeing see not; and hearing they hear not, neither do they understand.

It is obvious that Jesus, through his use of parables, is trying to convey truth through the Mysteries. As well, this also tells us that Jesus was initiated, probably in Egypt as a young man, at a Mystery school.

In the past the word "myth" did not refer to something false, as it is the case today. For most people, a myth was a pleasant story; to the initiated, it was a sacred code hiding profound spiritual teachings. The ancients did not believe that the Mystery myths were literally true; they were seen as the introduction to the profound mystical philosophy at the base of the Mysteries.

The Mysteries were divided in many levels of initiation that led progressively the initiates to ever-deeper levels of understanding. The number of levels was different in all Mystery traditions. They started with the Outer mysteries, in which myths are seen as religious stories, to the Inner mysteries, in which the myths are explained as spiritual allegories. The Mysteries were everywhere in the Pagan world and the most important one was Dionysus, god-man of the Eleusinian Mysteries, albeit under different names: in Greece (Dionysus), Italy (Bacchus), Egypt (Osiris), Asia Minor (Attis), Syria (Adonis), Persia (Mithras), etc. Spectacles were held representing the death and resurrection of their god-man.

Since the ancients believed that all the Mystery god-men were in fact the same mythic being, all the time they combined the different myths and rites to create new forms of the Mysteries that crossed national boundaries. For instance, in Alexandria, Timotheus combined Osiris and Dionysus to create a new deity that he called Serapis.

Jesus used the same methods taught to him at the Mystery schools. He taught using parables, whose real meanings were not apparent to the uninitiated, but were clear to the initiated that saw deeper meaning and understanding to the myths. This is in direct opposition to the modern day belief of many Christian churches who see the Bible and the teachings of Jesus as being literal. However, when you examine the Mysteries, you see that the Bible, especially the New Testament, was obviously written under this influence.

The Mysteries were divided into two general parts, the Less Mysteries and the Greater. The Less Mysteries were composed of dramatic rites or ceremonies, with some teaching; the Greater Mysteries were composed of, or conducted almost entirely on the ground of, study; and the doctrines taught in them later were proved by personal experience in initiation.

In the Greater Mysteries it was explained, among other things, the secret meaning of the mythologies of the old religions. This was incorporated into the teachings of Christianity, who used the ancient myths, to teach the ultimate truth. Unfortunately, the secret meanings of the Bible and the teachings of Jesus have been obscured by the parables and fables that are taken as literal truths, rather than as a fable meant to teach an abstract idea.

GNOSTICISM

Gnosticism is a dualistic religious and philosophical movement of the late Hellenistic and early Christian eras that became popular in the Roman world in the 2nd – 3rd century C.E. The term designates a wide assortment of Christian sects that promised salvation through an occult knowledge that they claimed was revealed to them alone. Scholars trace these salvation religions back to such diverse sources as Jewish mysticism, Hellenistic mystery cults, Iranian religious dualism, Babylonian and Egyptian mythology.

Gnosis, which translates as Knowledge, as a spiritual belief system, was present in earlier Greek and Egyptian philosophy. By the first century C.E. Christian ideas were incorporated into these syncretistic systems, and by the second century the largest of them, organized by Valentinus and Basilides, were a significant rival to Christianity.

Forbidden Magic Spells From The Bible

Some Gnostics taught that the world is ruled by evil archons, among them the deity of the Old Testament, who hold captive the spirit of humanity. The heavenly pleroma was the center of the divine life, and Jesus was interpreted as an intermediary eternal being, or aeon, sent from the pleroma to restore the lost knowledge of humanity's divine origin. Gnostics held secret formulas, which they believed would free them at death from the evil archons and restore them to their heavenly abode.

Gnosticism held that human beings consist of flesh, soul, and spirit (the divine spark), and that humanity is divided into classes representing each of these elements. The purely corporeal lacked spirit and could never be saved; Gnostics who understood the secret teaching bore the divine spark and their salvation was certain. Others, like the Christians, who stood in between, might attain a lesser salvation through faith.

Among some of the Gnostics, a priesthood of the mysteries existed and these initiated priests practiced magic, astrology, incantations, exorcisms, the fashioning of charms, talismans, and amulets. These priests were viewed as heretics by the church, which in the second and third century struggled to separate from them.

Upon gaining control of the Roman Empire, Christian leaders periodically, and often violently, suppressed Gnostic groups. Manicheism, a later movement of Gnosticism that emphasized its dualistic tendencies, was founded by a prophet named Mani (216-276 C.E.), who was noted for his skill in astrology, medicines, and magic.

The Carpocratians, one of the Gnostic sects, seem to have derived some of their mysteries and rites from Isis worship, and used theurgic incantations, symbols, and signs. The Ophites also adapted Egyptian rites, and, as their name indicates, these included serpent symbolism, an actual serpent being the central object of their mysteries.

Marcos, a disciple of Valentinus, and founder of the Marcian sect, reportedly celebrated Mass with two chalices, pouring wine from the larger into a smaller, and on pronouncing a magical formula, the vessel was filled with a liquor like blood. Other sects practiced divination and prophecy by using women psychics. Some of the sects engaged in rituals of a sexual nature.

The Gnostic talismans were mostly engraved on gems, the color and traditional qualities of the jewel being part of its magical efficacy. They used spells and charms and mystic formulas, said to "loose fetters, to cause blindness in one's enemies, to procure dreams, to gain favor, to encompass any desire whatsoever."

In a Greek Gnostic papyrus the following spell of Agathocles for producing dreams was found:

"Take a cat, black all over, and which has been killed; prepare a writing tablet, and write the following with a solution of myrrh, and the dream which thou desirest to be sent, and put in the mouth of the cat. The text to be transcribed runs: 'Keimi, Keimi, I am the Great One, in whose mouth rests Mommom, Thoth, Nauumbre, Karikha, Kenyro, Paarmiathon, the sacred Ian icê ieu aêoi, who is above the heaven, Amekheumen, Neunana, Seunana, Ablanathanalba. Put thyself in connection with N.N. in this matter, but if it is necessary then bring for me N.N. hither by thy power; lord of the whole world, fiery god, put thyself in connection with N.N....Hear me, for I shall speak the great name, Thoth! whom each god honors, and each demon fears, by whose command every messenger performs his mission. Thy name answers to the seven a, e, ê, i, o, u, ô, iauoeêaô ouȇ ôia. I named thy glorious name, the name for all needs. Put thyself in connection with N.N., Hidden One, God, with respect to this name, which Apollobex also used."

The repetition/chanting of various syllables, otherwise apparently meaningless, was always thought to be extremely effective in magical rites, either as holding the secret name of the powers invoked, or of actual power in themselves. Atanasi's Magic Papyrus, Spell VII directs one to place the link of a chain upon a leaden plate, and having traced its outline, to write around the circumference the common Gnostic legend in Greek characters (reading both ways) continuously.

Within the circle should be written the nature of what was to be prevented. The operation was called "The Ring of Hermes." The link was then to be folded up on the leaden plate, and thrown into the grave of one dead before his time, or else into a disused well. After the formula was to follow in Greek: "Prevent thou such and such a person from doing such and such a thing"— a proof that the string of epithets all referred to the same power.

These instances might be multiplied, although much of the Gnostic teachings were lost as the Gnostic lost out in the religious struggles of the era. Gnosticism was passed on through the centuries in various groups usually described as heretical groups such as the Cathars and Bogomils. It reemerged in the late Middle Ages in alchemy and with the rise of the Rosicrucians and nineteenth-century Theosophy.

Forbidden Magic Spells From The Bible

We can see that despite what the churches are teaching, there is a rich tradition of magical practices in Christianity that has remained hidden behind a veil of secrecy to this very day. However, some magic rituals are still an important part of most churches Sunday services. This would come as a surprise to their congregations who may not realize they are participating every week in something that supposedly is condemned by the church.

Forbidden Magic Spells From The Bible

II. Hidden Magic of the Bible

ALL RELIGIONS contain spoken and written spells in the form of prayers and blessed items. The Rosary is an enhancer, by which a person concentrates and focuses their attention on prayers which they repeat over and over again. This repetition accompanied by concentrating on one bead after another is in reality, a spell to awaken the inner consciousness to reach for God and higher inspiration. Prayer beads and wheels are used in other forms in Eastern, and other religions, as well as in Christianity.

The various medals upon which are inscribed Latin Phrases and images of Holy characters are talismans, or written spells, designed to focus the believer's attention on the Saint or Angel for the purpose of invoking the illustrious being to grant favors of protection, good fortune, healing, etc.

Saints' prayers often have coercive force, while magical charms and rituals have a supplicatory element. As well, Christianity shared many assumptions that were basic to a magical worldview. Primary among these was that of a vitalistic Universe divided into three levels, the super-celestial, celestial, and terrestrial, each of which was intimately linked to the others through a series of correspondences, sympathies, and antipathies that might be hidden (occult) but that were regular, rational, and discoverable.

Christianity and magic also agreed on the existence of invisible, spiritual entities (angels, demons, devils), who interacted with humans in many ways, including sexually. Christianity and magic both emphasized the power and efficacy of words, a belief that was intensified by the Christian reliance on the spoken and written word and by the notion of Christ as the incarnate word of God. Many magical prayers and formulas were simply adaptations of Christian formulations.

Forbidden Magic Spells From The Bible

A further link between Christianity and magic was the belief that hidden powers and virtues existed in natural objects (candles, incense, amulets, talismans, relics, holy water, the sign of the cross, the Eucharist, church bells), which could be tapped for human use. Given these similarities, one can conclude that throughout the century's magic often seems indistinguishable from religion.

In Lord Jesus' famous Sermon on the Mount, as recorded in St, Matthew's Gospel, chapter 5, 6 and 7, he gives unmistakable formulas of words and actions for dealing with the problems of life. Also, when asked, "Lord, teach us to pray" he gave us an actual spoken formula, embodied in "The Lord's Prayer."

Even though some misguided religious devotees condemn such practices as being of the devil, they are in fact using this practice, ignorant of that fact because of the misinformation they receive from their leaders.

Many people find comfort each day by reading the Biblical book of Psalms, yet, little do they know that this is a book of magical sacred spells, that when used in a certain manner, can work seeming miracles. The first thing to keep in mind is that there are many types of practices for inner development and personal power. In this work I have attempted to share the ones which I feel would be of the greatest benefit to the readers of this book.

The second thing to remember is that each spell described is a magnetic operation. By that I mean that it is designed to awaken latent powerful forces within the practitioner, to help bring about the desired results. Such magnetic operations should be prepared in secrecy and with reverence. If you tell anyone what you are doing it will cause some of your energy to be drained from this work, especially if they are an unbeliever in such things. Therefore, any effort you make to prepare correctly and work secretly will be greatly rewarded.

Do not do any of these things when you are angry or upset. Do not eat for a few hours before performing any practice described. The third thing to remember is that practice makes perfection. It will do no good just to read about these things, you must practice them. Do not be disappointed if your first attempts at Forbidden Magic Spells From The Bible do not succeed. Your mind must be clearly focused on what you are asking for. As well, if your spell does not seem to work, perhaps you should rethink what you are asking for.

Often the Universe has a path set out for you that you are required to follow, no matter what. By attempting a magical spell to counteract this path of destiny may interfere with an important aspect of your reason for being on this planet in the first place. Remember to try and look at the big picture rather than just the narrow viewpoint of your ego.

I have attempted to reveal the spells that require a minimum of preparation or materials. However, some of the rituals do call for using such objects as candles, incense and crystals. But do not let this frighten you away as Bible Spells can be performed by anyone.

You are to keep all of these things in a safe place, where they will stay clean and untouched by anyone else. Again I repeat, keep your work secret. If you must share this with anyone, be sure they are truly with you in your work and conviction.

It would be best if you have your own room to do these things that is totally private. However, if this is not the case, do not let that stop you from doing this work: just try to arrange things when you are alone, in any room that is convenient for you. Also, any table or shelf can become your altar, so long it is clean.

Finally, and most important, remember that this work is between you and God. You are working towards a goal, so believe in its importance and keep the faith. Your success or failure depends on your constant effort and faith. Be patient, it took some time for you to become the person that you are with your strong and weak points, so allow for some time to change things. How long it takes once you begin depends on your relationship with the higher powers of life. Therefore, strive to be in harmony with all forms of life as much as possible.

In some of the spells it is required that you speak unusual words; I have tried to illustrate their sounds as simply as possible, but if you still have a problem pronouncing them, then just repeat them mentally, although they are more effective when spoken aloud.

THE POWER AND SYMBOLISM OF CANDLES

Many of the Bible-based spells in this book involve the use of candles. Candle magic has a long and interesting history behind it all on its own. However, when teamed up with Bible-based magic, the power and symbolism of candle magic takes on a whole new intensity that resonates with the powers of Divine Creation. Part of this strength comes from the candle's flame; fire holds a special place in all forms of magic because it contains the spark of divinity which shines within us and in all living things. Fire carries within it the spark of creation, something it shares with all living things.

Ancient Pagans used candles and lamps in religious observances. Early Christianity shunned the use of lights, because of the popularity of honoring the divine with light was viewed as pagan. Indeed, the Greek funeral custom was to accompany the dead with torchlight or candlelight so that the soul of the dying could not be seized by demons.

Many church leaders in the first three centuries of Christianity spoke openly about the disdain they had for candles and lights. At this time Rome also had a competing salvation religion that centered on the Egyptian goddess, Isis. The followers of Isis kept her temple lamps lit at all hours, both day and night, to symbolize constant hope. Despite the fact that Christ called himself the "Light of the World," the early Christians resisted adopting anything obliquely seen as pagan into their religion.

Nevertheless, by the fourth century, both candles and lamps were part of Christian rituals, but it was not until the latter part of the Middle Ages, from the twelfth century on, that candles were placed on church altars. The Catholic Church established the use of consecrated holy candles in rituals of blessings and absolving sins, and in exorcizing demons.

From the early days of the Church symbols were ways of communicating with people of the same beliefs without fear of persecution, and many of our religious candles reflect this early symbolism. New symbolism of candles and flames emerged to coincide with church beliefs. Primarily the focus was on beeswax symbolizing the virgin mother, the wick symbolizing the soul of Jesus Christ, and the flame representing the Divinity which absorbs and dominates both.

The word ceremony comes from the Latin word cermonius, meaning "the person who carries a wax candle at public rituals." Pope Gelasius in the fifth century established a feast day called Candlemas, during which all of the church's candles were blessed, though the blessing of the candles did not come into common use until the eleventh century. In Dorsetshire England, the custom of giving the poorer tradesmen a large candle at Candlemas continued up to the 20th century.

Forbidden Magic Spells From The Bible

COLORS

It is commonly known within metaphysical circles that color plays a great part in healing work. It is also known that a specific color can trigger a psychic response from the subconscious mind as a means of tapping the inner power to accomplish a chosen purpose.

Color has been applied to candle burning for centuries in one form or another. There are many theories as to which color candle to use for a given purpose. Most of these theories agree, but some may contradict the others. However, for the purpose of clarity in the present work, we have broken down the candle color and purpose correspondence in a simplified form.

RED: Energy or Love

PINK: Love

Green: Money and Good Fortune

Blue: Healing or Psychic Development

Purple: Power over Enemies, Personal Power, Spiritual Attainment, to Rid or Prevent Bad Luck and Curses

WHITE: Use this color to substitute any other color

INCENSE

Burning incense is a tradition that dates back thousands of years, in practically all of earth's ancient civilizations, and is well known for its mood-altering qualities. The word Incense is derived from the Latin verb incendere, "to burn."

It has been used to accompany prayer, to worship the Gods, purify the air, release negative vibrations, induce self-awareness and to uplift the emotional state. There are many references to incense in the Old and New Testament and the Roman Catholics still use incense at mass and in many other of their rituals. It symbolizes the sacredness of a person or occasion, and their prayer as it rises to God. When incense is burned before magical workings, fragrant smoke also purifies the surrounding area of negative, disturbing vibrations. Though such purification isn't usually necessary, it helps create the appropriate mental state necessary for the successful practice of magic.

Forbidden Magic Spells From The Bible

When the incense is smoldered in a ritual setting it undergoes a transformation. The vibrations, no longer trapped in their physical form, are released into the environment. Their energies, mixing with those who use them, speed out to effect the changes necessary to the manifestation of the magical goal. Each different fragrance has its own vibration, so incense can be selected to assist with mood enhancement, to help you feel good; soothing and uplifting – to reduce stressful situations, and to assist with personal development. It is also excellent to burn while saying affirmations, to raise your consciousness and purify the atmosphere in which you live.

Most people choose their incense "from their heart," thus allowing for intuition to guide them for their "highest good." Therefore, incense plays a very important role in creating a healthy environment in which those people seeking wisdom and truth can tune in' to their purpose in life.

A simplified list of incense for Bible-based magic is as follows:

Frankincense: Draw upon the energy of the sun to create sacred space, consecrate objects, and stimulate positive vibrations

Jasmine: For luck in general, especially in matters relating to love

Musk: Burn for courage and vitality, or to heighten sensual passion

Myrrh: Ancient incense for protection, healing, purification, spirituality, and to remove bad luck and curses

Patchouli: An earthy scent used in money and attraction spells

Pine: Burn for strength, and to reverse negative energies

Rose: For love magic, and to return calm energies to the home

Sandalwood: An all purpose scent that can also be used to heal and protect, also for purification

CRYSTALS AND GEMSTONES

Another excellent way to add energy to your Bible-based magic is to include a crystal or gemstone along with your spell. Crystals and gemstones contain powerful earth energies which can help balance and heal psychological, emotional and physical ailments. Imbalances of the energy field within and surrounding us are often the cause or contributing factor to illness and disease. If you are not properly balanced and energized, then any attempted magic will be ineffective. Crystals help harmonize the emotions and help recover from difficult mental states. Energy flow can be balanced and corrected so that health can be restored on all levels.

It is not necessary to look beyond your own favorite quartz crystal to aid in your Bible-based magic. Quartz provides clarity of vision, protection, peace, purity, life force, relieving of pain, self, innocence, meditation, truth, forms of healing, psychic matters, purification, beginning a new phase, and is an all purpose crystal. If you do not have access to other types of gemstones, a quartz crystal can be used for any Bible-based magic.

It must be made clear that any crystal is a tool, it will not make you rich, beautiful, healthy, etc. It can assist you in making your goals a reality, but you have to be working towards it. Each crystal is like a battery—storing and releasing energy at a specific frequency. When you need energy, it will give it. When you need to have energies removed, it will take them away. With that in mind, here are the basics in crystal magic:

In meditation: Using crystals in mediation is easy. Simply hold the crystal in your hand, wear it around your neck or place it close to you while you meditate. It can add its energies to yours, open new doorways, etc.

In ritual: Crystals can be used to represent the elements. They can be used to add energy to spellwork, placed at various points around your magic circle to protect, or used to remove negative energies.

Every day: The easiest way to use the power of crystals is to wear them. Whether it is in a necklace, a ring, or a bracelet, keeping the crystal close to your skin will allow it to work with you all day long. Crystals make excellent amulets and can be charged with very specific purposes (such as protection). Another way to use them is to keep them close to areas that you frequent. Place crystals by your bed, under your pillow, in your office, in your car, in your purse, where ever you may need them. If you are interested in using other types of gemstones with your Bible magic, here is a simple list of suggested stones.

Healing/Health: Agate, amber, amethyst, aventurine, azurite, bloodstone, calcite, carnelian, cat's eye, celestite, chrysoprase, coral, quartz crystal, diamond, flint, garnet, hematite, holey stones, jade, jasper, jet, lapis lazuli, peridot, petrified wood, pyrite, sapphire, sodalite, staurolite, sugilite, sulfur, sunstone, topaz, turquoise, red zircon.

Forbidden Magic Spells From The Bible

Love: Agate, alexandrite, amber, amethyst, beryl, calcite, chrysocolla, emerald, jade, lapis lazuli, lepidolite, malachite, moonstone, olivine, pearl, rhodocrosite, rose quartz, sapphire, topaz, pink tourmaline, turquoise.

Money, Wealth, Prosperity: Aventurine, bloodstone, calcite, cat's-eye, chrysoprase, coal, emerald, jade, mother-of-pearl, olivine, opal, pearl, peridot, ruby, salt, sapphire, spinel, staurolite, tiger's-eye, topaz, green tourmaline, brown-green-red zircon.

Good Luck/Remove Bad Luck and Curses, Protection: Apache Tear, carnelian, cat's-eye, citrine, chrysoprase, lepidolite, malachite, moonstone, obsidian, opal, peridot, sardonyx, staurolite, topaz, turquoise.

The Egyptians used crystals in their secret funeral ceremonies and in their magical cult practices. They assigned symbolic power meanings to crystals and gemstones that gave the stones a value that exceeded their simple mineral origins. The meanings associated with them were for health, protection in life and the afterlife, and good fortune, just to name a few. The famous golden funerary mask of King Tutankhamen, which is around 3,500 years old, contains many crystals and gemstones, including Obsidian, Calcite, Carnelian, Green feldspar (Amazonite), Malachite and Lapis Lazuli.

Gemstones with mystic powers are referred to several times in the Bible. Twelve "Sacred Stones of Fire" were originally guarded by Lucifer (Ezekiel 28:13) – "You were in Eden, The garden of God; every precious gem adorned you..." However, tradition says that they were taken back on his downfall.

The stones were later given to Moses who was told to set them in the breastplate of his brother Aaron, the high priest (Exodus 28:15-30).

The gems were set in four rows of three. The first row was Sardius (thought to be Carnelian), Topaz and Carbuncle (Ruby). The second row – Emerald, Sapphire and Diamond. The third row – Ligure (Rubellite), Agate and Amethyst. The fourth row – Beryl, Onyx and Jasper.

Throughout history, precious stones have held a mystical power over royalty and commoner alike who valued both their beauty and the symbolic power meanings they represented. They have a unique quality that inspires some people to exceed their own human abilities and limitations by providing them with an esoteric power that they believe operates on their behalf.

III. Secrets of the Verses

IN THIS chapter I will demonstrate the power contained within Bible verses. It is advised that the reader practice first with the simple spells from this chapter in order to better understand the amazing energies that can be used from Bible-based magic.

One of the most important ingredients for working magic is will power. The most important preparation for magic is mental preparation. You must train yourself to focus exclusively on the object of your desire – your reason for working the magic.

One of the secrets to successful magic is to see the finished product – to concentrate on the end result rather than on the steps to getting there. You would concentrate on the situation as it will be when the magic has done its work.

Close your eyes and breathe slowly, deeply and rhythmically until you feel completely relaxed. Imagine yourself surrounded by white light, enclosed in a bright bubble of energy or otherwise protected from harm. If it makes you more comfortable call upon God, your guardian angel, spirit guide, or patron saint to be with you in this work.

Before doing any type of Bible-based magic, you should also check on the phase of the Moon. Of all the planets, the Moon's influence on subtle energies is the strongest. Subtle power increases as the Moon waxes, so the time of the waxing Moon is best for spells involving growth or increase, such as money spells. The power peaks when the Moon is full and that is the best time for workings of culmination and love. During the waning Moon, power subsides and turns inward. The waning Moon's period is used for banishing, bindings, and discovering hidden secrets.

Forbidden Magic Spells From The Bible

No magic spell is going to bring results unless channels are opened into the material world. For example, a job spell is useless if you are not willing to go out and interview for jobs or at least let potential employers know that you are in the market for one. In the same vein, a healing spell is no substitute for proper medical care.

Visualization used in creating a Bible verse spell should focus on the desired result, not the individual steps leading up to the result. We give the spell free rein in how it goes about achieving the results with the understanding that it is not to bring harm to anyone. For this reason, spells have a habit of working in unexpected ways.

To assure that the power we have unleashed does not inadvertently cause harm, we bind the spell. This serves to "set" the form we have created so that the energy becomes fixed in the pattern we desire. The energy we project to others affects us even more strongly than the other person. This is because we have generated the energy, and thus we have become the object at which the energy is directed. If healing energy is sent out, then the health of the person casting the spell is enhanced. By the same token, any hex or curse that is sent out always affects the person who sends it no matter whether it affected the person it was sent at or not.

Bible-based magic is not to be used to gain power over others. Magic is a technique used in developing your own power from within. Spells that are directed at gaining power over others weaken the power from within. Once you have cast the Bible verse spell, do not discuss it with any one until after it has worked.

Most spells run out of energy because the person who cast it talks about it to other people. Because of this, the spell is robbed of power before it has a chance to work. So in order for the energies of Creation to work, keep silent. Above all, at all times, remember that your Bible-based magic is not to be used to harm anyone or to cause anyone to do something against their will.

A SIMPLE BEGINNING

For our first foray into Bible-based magic, we shall start with a few simple but tried and true Bible spells in order to familiarize you with the method. As you become more familiar with Bible-based magic, you can attempt some of the more complex spells that use candles or crystals. But for now, let's take things slowly.

As with any kind of magic, you first have to get yourself in the right state of mind. You want to have a quiet, private location to work your spell. It is imperative that you can spend at least a half an hour by yourself without any interruptions.

You next want to clearly envision what your spell is going to accomplish. This is extremely important, for unless you have a clear goal in mind, your spell will be useless. This is what ultimately dooms most spells to failure – the inability to clearly and concisely envision what your need is.

The human mind has an unpleasant habit of not being able to hold its attention on any one subject for more than a few seconds at a time. Our thoughts tend to constantly jump around from one issue to another, never allowing our consciousness to focus on one idea or desire for any length of time. This is why learning how to meditate is an excellent practice for anyone wishing to learn to practice magic.

So take some time to meditate on what it is you wish to accomplish with your magic spell. Another good method is to write down what you want to happen with your spell.

Take a plain piece of white paper and write down your desire or need. Keep it simple, and state clearly what it is you want to happen.

For example, if you are looking for a new job, write down: "I will soon find a new and better job."

Don't write: "I wish I could find a new and better job."

You have to make a statement on what you want to happen. Not a wish. You are telling the Universe that you <u>WILL</u> find a new job.

The same goes for a love and romance spell. Write down: "I will soon find a new and better love." Once again, don't put down: "I wish that I could find a new and better love." You have to use your powers of creation to make your desire happen by focusing on what <u>WILL</u> happen. Not by focusing on wishing something to happen.

Also, don't hope for something to happen. Don't write down, or concentrate on "hoping" something will happen. You have to <u>COMMAND</u> it to happen.

Forbidden Magic Spells From The Bible

God the Creator did not say: "I hope there will be light." He said: "Let there be light!" And it was so. Since you are a part of creation, you have also been given the powers of Creation. When you cast your spell, you are using your abilities to CREATE your desires. So don't play around, state clearly and with confidence what you want.

"I WILL find true love!" "I WILL get a new and better job!" "I WILL make more money!" "I WILL have good luck!"

Find out what you want to happen in your life, and then do it!

Now that you have established what it is that you want, and you have focused exclusively on this desire, it is time to bring into play the power of Bible-based magic. I have chosen for you three simple verses from the Bible that address the three most common desires that people use magic for: Love -- Money – Good luck.

Let us first start with love. Focus on your desire for love and romance. Now, repeat out loud the following Bible verse three times and repeat for three days at the same time each day:

"Many waters cannot quench love; rivers cannot wash it away. If one were to give all the wealth of his house for love, it would be utterly scorned."

(Song of Solomon 8:7)

A new romance will begin within three weeks.

Now let's try a money spell. We all have times when money is a little tight, so let's do a Bible Verse spell to bring in a small amount of money.

Again, concentrate, or write down what you want to occur: "I WILL get enough money to tide me over."

You may also want to add a stipulation that this money is only to come to you without harming anyone else in the process. After all, money does not grow on trees, it has to come from somewhere, and you don't want to take something that doesn't rightfully belong to you and belongs to someone else

Forbidden Magic Spells From The Bible

As with the love spell, focus on your desire for a little extra money. Now, repeat out loud the following Bible verse three times and repeat for three days at the same time each day:

"Charge them that are rich in this world, that they be not highminded, nor trust in uncertain riches, but in the living God, who giveth us richly all things to enjoy; That they do good, that they be rich in good works, ready to distribute, willing to communicate; Laying up in store for themselves a good foundation against the time to come, that they may lay hold on eternal life."

(1 Timothy 6:17-19)

Money will arrive within three weeks.

Finally we will try out the good luck spell. We all have times when we feel as if good luck has simply disappeared from our lives. As the song goes: "If it weren't for bad luck I'd have no luck at all," I am sure that we all have had this feeling where it seems that bad luck has taken over and that good fortune has left us high and dry.

With this spell you state: "I <u>WILL</u> have good luck from now on!" You want to avoid saying something like: "I WILL no longer have bad luck!" Your objective is to create GOOD LUCK. By mentioning bad luck in any capacity in your spell can give energy where it does not belong. You always want the emphasis the positive and ignore the negative.

One word of warning where it comes to good and bad luck – Karma is a very powerful force in the cosmos and good and bad luck tend to go hand in hand. You might want to consider why you are experiencing bad luck at the moment. Think long and hard on the direction that you are taking your life. Often the Universe tries to guide us towards the life that we are suppose to lead by putting up "road block" when we stray off of our intended path. You do not want to ask for good luck if it reinforces your bad choices in life.

You might want to add a small caveat in your spell by stating: "I <u>WILL</u> have good luck if I am on the correct path!" This way you are helping create a good future for yourself if you are living your life the way that you intended when you made your pre-birth spiritual agreement.

Forbidden Magic Spells From The Bible

As before, focus on your desire for good luck. Now, repeat out loud the following Bible verse three times and repeat for three days at the same time each day:

"We know that in everything God works for good with those who love him, who are called according to his purpose."

(Romans 8:28)

Good luck will arrive within three weeks.

You will find that unlike the three simple examples, a number of Bible Verse spells use verses that have a long and secret tradition for magical practices. These verses may seem like they have no connection with the type of magical spell you are trying to cast, but be assured that each verse in this book is highly powerful and effective for your needs.

Forbidden Magic Spells From The Bible

IV. Folk Magic and Secret Traditions

SECRET SPELLS taken from the Bible has been used for centuries by practitioners of various forms of what is known as folk magic. Other names of this type of magic are hoodoo, pow-wow, braucha and conjuring.

It is thought that folk magic came from the Pennsylvania Dutch who brought from Germany their extensive heritage of ancient magical practices based on the Bible and Jewish Kaballah. The basic Pennsylvania Dutch Hex premise – that is somewhat at odds with the typical relationship of Christians to their God—is that we are co-creators with the Deity of that which manifests. Subtle changes here and now can work miracles down the road, if properly applied. Folk magic is a traditional collection of European magic spells, recipes, and folk remedies mixed from Roman Catholic prayers, magic words, and simple rituals to cure simple domestic ailments and rural troubles.

Folk magic has also combined a large body of African folklore practices and beliefs with a considerable admixture of American Indian botanical knowledge. The mountainous regions of the American south have been a treasure trove of folk magic beliefs and practices, but you can find folk magic traditions in most rural areas all across the United States.

HEALING WITH BIBLE VERSES

When it comes to healing, those who practice Bible-based magic are practitioners of God's healing power, intermediaries through which God cures the faithful. Therefore, a person must believe not only in God the creator, but also in the ability of the practitioner to be assured of a cure. Psalm 50/15 is the Bible verse that is considered to be the basis for the practice of Bible magic: "Call upon me in the day of trouble: I will deliver thee and thou shalt glorify me."

Forbidden Magic Spells From The Bible

Undoubtedly, one of the most valuable abilities of a Bible Verse spell is the method to stop uncontrollable bleeding. In the days before modern medicine uncontrollable bleeding could lead to a quick death for a person or farm animal alike. Even in this day and age, the ability to stop bleeding, especially from a distance, should be considered essential learning to a healer.

There are a number of different methods that have been handed down from Mother to son, Father to daughter. The most common involves the reading aloud the sixth verse of the sixteenth chapter of the book of Ezekiel:

"And when I passed by thee, and saw thee polluted in thine own blood, I said unto thee when thou wast in thy blood, Live; yea, I said unto thee when thou vast in thy blood, Live."

When reading the verse, however, always substitute the victim's name for the word "thee" when it appeared in the verse.

If you are doing this method from a distance, a river or creek in between you and your subject can act as interference, causing the healing energies you are sending to be diverted downstream. In this case, it is best to take yourself to a quiet room with your Bible and meditate on this verse in order to add extra energy to your healing spell. The stronger the flow of water, the more energy you will need to succeed.

Another good remedy to stop bleeding is to say these words out loud three times:

This is the day on which the injury happened. Blood, thou must stop, until the Virgin Mary brings forth another son.

Then repeat three times the name of the person bleeding.

The following Bible Verses are to be used for healing. The best method is to repeat each verse three times; followed by the name of the person (or pet) you are attempting to heal. This should be done for three days in a row.

Forbidden Magic Spells From The Bible

For extra healing energies, take yourself to a quiet room, free from distractions and interruptions. After repeating your spell, spend about fifteen minutes in quiet contemplation of the verse and the person you are trying to heal.

HEALING DISEASE ASSOCIATED WITH OLD AGE

Psalm 103:2-5

Praise the LORD, O my soul, and forget not all his benefits- who forgives all your sins and heals all your diseases, who redeems your life from the pit and crowns you with love and compassion, who satisfies your desires with good things so that your youth is renewed like the eagle's.

HEALING DEPRESSION AND ANXIETY

Psalm 147:1-3

Praise the LORD. How good it is to sing praises to our God, how pleasant and fitting to praise him!

The LORD builds up Jerusalem; he gathers the exiles of Israel. He heals the brokenhearted and binds up their wounds.

HEALING STOMACH AND EATING DISORDERS

Matthew 7:7-11

Ask and it will be given to you; seek and you will find; knock and the door will be opened to you. For everyone who asks receives; he who seeks finds; and to him who knocks, the door will be opened. Which of you, if his son asks for bread, will give him a stone? 10Or if he asks for a fish, will give him a snake? 11If you, then, though you are evil, know how to give good gifts to your children, how much more will your Father in heaven give good gifts to those who ask him!

HEALING ALCOHOLISM

Mark 16:17-18

And these signs will follow those who believe: In My name they will cast out demons, they will speak with new tongues, they will take up serpents; and if they drink anything deadly they will recover; they will lay hands on the sick, and they will recover.

HEALING COLD, FLU AND LUNG PROBLEMS

John 16:23-24

In that day you will no longer ask me anything. I tell you the truth, my Father will give you whatever you ask in my name. Until now you have not asked for anything in my name. Ask and you will receive, and your joy will be complete.

HEALING ARTHRITIS AND BONE DISEASES

2 Corinthians 1:19-20

For the Son of God, Jesus Christ, who was preached among you by me and Silas and Timothy, was not "Yes" and "No," but in him it has always been "Yes." For no matter how many promises God has made, they are "Yes" in Christ. And so through him the "Amen" is spoken by us to the glory of God.

HEALING OF HIGH BLOOD PRESSURE

Acts 4:29-31

Now, Lord, consider their threats and enable your servants to speak your word with great boldness. Stretch out your hand to heal and perform miraculous signs and wonders through the name of your holy servant Jesus. After they prayed, the place where they were meeting was shaken. And they were all filled with the Holy Spirit and spoke the word of God boldly.

Forbidden Magic Spells From The Bible

HEALING OF SEXUAL DYSFUNCTIONS

Galatians 3:29

And now that you belong to Christ, you are the true children of Abraham. You are his heirs, and now all the promises God gave to him belong to you.

HEALING OF KIDNEY AND BACK PAIN

Hebrews 9:14

How much more, then, will the blood of Christ, who through the eternal Spirit offered himself unblemished to God, cleanse our consciences from acts that lead to death, so that we may serve the living God!

HEALING FROM INFECTIONS

Hebrews 10:22

Let us draw near to God with a sincere heart in full assurance of faith, having our hearts sprinkled to cleanse us from a guilty conscience and having our bodies washed with pure water.

HEALING FOR ANY KIND OF SICKNESS

James 5:14-16

Is any one of you sick? He should call the elders of the church to pray over him and anoint him with oil in the name of the Lord. And the prayer offered in faith will make the sick person well; the Lord will raise him up. If he has sinned, he will be forgiven. Therefore confess your sins to each other and pray for each other so that you may be healed. The prayer of a righteous man is powerful and effective.

HEALING FROM WARTS AND OTHER GROWTHS

1 John 1:9 - If we confess our sins, he is faithful and just and will forgive us our sins and purify us from all unrighteousness

HEALING FROM INJURIES AND CHRONIC PAIN

1 Peter 2:24

He himself bore our sins in his body on the tree, that we might die to sins and live for righteousness; by his wounds, you have been healed.

Other healing chants can be said without accompanying Bible verses. It is recommended that before each chant, one should spend some time quietly reading the Bible, thinking about the person who is to be healed, and their illness or injury.

These chants, while they seem old fashioned and simplistic, have been handed down from generation to generation due to their effectiveness. The tradition of these spells stem from the fiftieth Psalm, according to Luther's translation: "Call upon me in the day of trouble; I will deliver thee, and thou shalt glorify me." In the Catholic translation, the same passage is found in the forty-ninth Psalm, reading thus: "Call upon me in the day of thy trouble, and I will deliver thee, and thou shalt glorify me."

WHEN ANYONE IS SICK

A remedy to be applied when anyone is sick, which has affected many a cure where doctors could not help. Let the sick person, without having conversed with anyone, put water in a bottle before sunrise, close it up tight, and put it immediately in some box or chest. Lock it and stop up the keyhole; the key must be carried one of the pockets for three days, as nobody dare have it except the person who puts the bottle with water in the chest or box.

REMEDY FOR WORMS, FOR PEOPLE OR ANIMALS

Mary, God's Mother, traversed the land,

Holding three worms close in her hand;

One was white, the other was black, the third was red.

This must be repeated three times, at the same time stroking the person or animal with the hand; and at the end of each application strike the back of the person or the animal, to wit: at the first application once, at the second application twice, and at the third application three times; and then set the worms a certain time, but not less than three minutes.

REMEDY FOR THE COLIC

I warn ye, ye colic fiends! There is one sitting in judgment, who speaketh: just or unjust. Therefore beware, ye colic fiends!

REMEDY FOR THE FEVER

Good morning, dear Thursday! Take away from [name] the 77-fold fevers. Oh! thou dear Lord Jesus Christ, take them away from him! This must be used on Thursday for the first time, on Friday for the second time, and on Saturday for the third time; and each time thrice.

The prayer of faith has also to be said each time, and not a word dare be spoken to anyone until the sun has risen. Neither dare the sick per, son speak to anyone till after sunrise; nor eat pork, nor drink milk, nor cross a running water, for nine days.

REMEDY FOR PALPITATION OF THE HEART

Palpitation and hide-bound, be off [name] ribs,

Since Christ, our Lord, spoke truth with his lips.

A SAFE REMEDY FOR VARIOUS ULCERS, BOILS AND OTHER DEFECTS

Take the root of an iron-weed, and tie it around the neck; it cures running ulcers; it also serves against obstructions in the bladder (stranguary), and cures the piles, if the roots are boiled in water with honey, and drank; it cleans and heals the lungs and affects a good breath. If this root is planted among grape vines or fruit trees, it promotes the growth very much. Children who carry it are educated without any difficulty; they become fond of all useful arts and sciences, and grow up joyfully and cheerfully.

GREAT POWER TO PREVENT WICKED OR MALICIOUS PERSONS FROM DOING YOU AN INJURY

Dullix, ix, ux. Yea, you can't come over Pontio; Pontio is above Pilato.

REMEDY FOR MORTIFICATION AND INFLAMMATION.

Sanctus Itorius res, call the rest. Here the mother of God came to his assistance, reaching out her snow-white hand, against the hot and cold brand.

Make three crosses with the thumb. Everything which is applied in words must be applied three times, and an interval of several hours must intervene each time, and for the third time it is to be applied the next day, unless where it is otherwise directed.

REMEDY FOR BAD WOUNDS AND BURNS

The word of God, the milk of Jesus' mother, and Christ's blood, is for all wounds and burnings good.

It is the safest way in all these cases to make the crosses with the hand or thumb three times over the affected parts; that is to say, over all those things to which the three crosses are attached.

TO STOP PAINS OR SMARTING IN A WOUND

Cut three small twigs from a tree—each to be cut off in one cut—rub one end of each twig in the wound, and wrap them separately in a piece of white paper, and put them in a warm and dry place.

TO BANISH THE WHOOPING COUGH

Cut three small bunches of hair from the crown of the head of a child that has never seen its father; sew this hair up in an unbleached rag and hang it around the neck of the child having the whooping cough. The thread with which the rag is sewed must also be unbleached.

ANOTHER REMEDY FOR THE WHOOPING COUGH

Thrust the child having the whooping cough three times through a blackberry bush, without speaking or saying anything. The bush, however, must be grown fast at the two ends, and the child must be thrust through three times in the same manner, that is to say, from the same side it was thrust through in the first place.

REMEDY FOR A TOOTHACHE

Stir the sore tooth with a needle until it draws blood; then take a thread and soak it with this blood. Then take vinegar and flour, mix them well so as to form a paste and spread it on a rag, then wrap this rag around the root of an apple-tree, and tie it very close with the above thread, after which the root must be well covered with ground.

REMEDY FOR BURNS

"Burn, I blow on thee!"— It must be blown on three times in the same breath, like the fire by the sun.

TO REMOVE BRUISES AND PAINS

Bruise, thou shalt not heat;

Bruise, thou shalt not sweat;

Bruise, thou shalt not run,

No-more than Virgin Mary shall bring forth another son.

TO CURE FITS OR CONVULSIONS

You must go upon another person's land, and repeat the following words: "I go before another court—I tie up my 77-fold fits."

Then cut three small twigs off any tree on the land; in each twig you must make a knot. This must be done on a Friday morning before sunrise, in the decrease of the moon unbeshrewdly. Then over your body where you feel the fits you make the crosses. And thus they may be made in all cases where they are applied.

TO BANISH CONVULSIVE FEVERS

Write the following letters on a piece of white paper, sew it on a piece of linen or muslin, and bang it around the neck until the fever leaves:

A b a x a C a t a b a x

A b a x a C a t a b a x

A b a x a C a t a b a

A b a x a C a t a b

A b a x a C a t a

A b a x a C a t

A b a x a C a

A b a x a C

A b a x a

A b a x

A b a

A b

Forbidden Magic Spells From The Bible

CURE FOR THE HEADACHE

Tame thou flesh and bone, like Christ in Paradise; and who will assist thee, this I tell thee [name] for your repentance sake.

This you must say three times, each time lasting for three minutes, and your headache will soon cease. But if your headache is caused by strong drink, or otherwise will not leave you soon, then you must repeat those words every minute. This, however, is not often necessary in regard to headache.

Forbidden Magic Spells From The Bible

V. The Magic Flame

A great soul once asked: "Why curse the darkness when you can light a candle?" The ritualistic burning of candles is a form of prayer, which can be performed in a complex and elaborate manner, or in the simplest form.

In this chapter we will explore only the simplified forms of candle magic because we are combining the magical art of candle burning with the invocation of Divine words and the power of Forbidden Bible Magic. This extremely powerful combination will serve the practitioner as a most powerful tool for dealing with the problems of life.

Before you begin, two things must be considered for your spell: Do you wish to attract, or repel? When you want to attract a certain thing into your life such as healing, good fortune, money, love, etc., you must prepare the candle by applying oil to it as you hold a mental picture of your desire. Some use olive oil, others use special purpose oil for anointing candles which can be obtained from spiritual/new age supply stores.

To anoint a candle to attract, the practitioner must apply some oil to the bottom of the candle on one side, then rub upward and stop at the center. Then one applies oil to the top of the candle, rub downward and stop at the same center spot.

When you wish to repel something from your life, such as psychic attack, ill fortune, undesirable conditions and situations etc., apply oil as follows: Apply some oil to the center of the candle on one side, then rub downward to the bottom. Then apply oil to the same center spot and rub upward to the tip of the candle. Remember, it is best to use only one candle for each purpose. Once you prepare a candle for a special purpose, do not use that candle for any other reason.

Forbidden Magic Spells From The Bible

When the candle has burned down to a stub, you should dispose of it properly. Some wrap the leftover wax in a piece of cloth and bury it. Others prefer to throw it into running water. Others throw the entire wax into a larger fire so that all is consumed. You may select the method that suits you.

Depending on what it is that you hope to achieve with your spell, choose an appropriately colored candle. Remember, if you only have one color of candle, a white candle can be used for any type of spell.

Decide if your spell is supposed to attract or repel. You then need to anoint the candle and carve upon it the Divine Name of Power based on attraction or repelling. To carve the Divine Names of Power on candles is a form of silent invocation to the power within that name.

Since the fall of man, Angelic Beings have communicated to the human race certain formulas by which humanity could regain the lost power of its original state. One such communication is Divine Names of Power meant to illuminate the mystical process. The Divine Names of Power are hidden within the Scriptures, and when written or spoken in a certain way, release an awesome power for great accomplishments.

One Divine Name of Power will attract, the other name is to repel. The Divine Name for attraction is: **SCHADDEI**. The Divine Name for repelling is: **AHA HE**.

I recommend that you use something made of clean metal to carve the Divine Name of Power. An unused pin or needle works well. If your candle is large enough, a sharp knife can be used. It is best not to repeat the Divine Names of Power out loud, unless you are able to pronounce them in the Hebrew language correctly.

After you have prepared your candle and carved the Divine Name of Power, the practitioner must then light the candle and begin the ritual. As always, choose to do your Bible Verse spell in a quiet location free of any distractions.

The first step of the ritual is to repeat the prescribed Bible verse out loud. What follows should be a sincere prayer, asking for the desired help in accomplishing your special purpose. Be sure to pray in your own words, for then the prayer will come from the heart.

Finally, one should remain in silent meditation on desired results for a few moments before closing the ritual. As you select the various Bible Verses to improve your condition, you must do so with a feeling of expectancy and an attitude of faith that you will receive the desired help from the universal Creative Force.

When you complete your session, do not think too much about it or worry as to how your help will come. Just be at ease, trying to be aware of opportunities that may arise in your daily life. Repeat a ritual for a specific purpose as often as possible, until you see the desired results. Keep a positive attitude and speak in a more positive manner.

Allow the candle to burn completely out and dispose of it properly. This will signify the end of your spell.

TO HAVE GOOD LUCK

Prepare a green candle to attract.

He is the image of the invisible God, the firstborn of all creation. For by him all things were created, in heaven and on earth, visible and invisible, whether thrones or dominions or rulers or authorities—all things were created through him and for him.
Colossians 1:15-16

NEW LOVE AND ROMANCE

Prepare a pink candle to attract.

Fear not, for I am with you;

be not dismayed, for I am your God;

I will strengthen you, I will help you,

I will uphold you with my righteous right hand.

Isaiah 41:10

GOOD FORTUNE IN BUSINESS AND MONEY

Prepare a green candle to attract.

God is not man, that he should lie,

or a son of man, that he should change his mind.

Has he said, and will he not do it?

Or has he spoken, and will he not fulfill it?

Numbers 23:19

KEEP SOMEONE AWAY

Prepare a purple candle to repel.

For am I now seeking the approval of man, or of God?

Or am I trying to please man? If I were still trying to please man,

I would not be a servant of Christ.

Galatians 1:10

TO ATTRACT GOOD HEALTH

Prepare a blue candle to attract.

I said to the boastful, 'Do not deal boastfully,' And to the wicked, 'Do not lift up the horn, Do not lift up your horn on high; Do not speak with a stiff neck,'" For exaltation comes neither from the east Nor from the west nor from the south, But God is the Judge: He puts down one, And exalts another.

Psalm 75:4-7

TO SEND AWAY BAD HEALTH

Prepare a white candle to repel.

Do not think that I came to destroy the Law or the Prophets; I did not come to destroy but to fulfill; For assuredly, I say to you, till heaven and earth pass away, one jot or one tittle will by no means pass from the law till all is fulfilled.

Matthew 5:17-18

PROTECTION WHILE TRAVELING

Prepare a purple candle to repel.

He drew a circular horizon on the face of the waters, At the boundary of light and darkness, The pillars of heaven tremble.

Job 26:10-14

TO RID YOURSELF OF A BOTHERSOME LOVER

Prepare a pink candle to repel.

May the glory of the Lord endure forever; May the Lord rejoice in His works, He looks on the earth, and it trembles; He touches the hills, and they smoke" I will sing to the Lord as long as I live; I will sing praise to my God while I have my being.

Psalms 104:31-33

TO GAIN TRUST AND FAVOR

Prepare a white candle to attract.

For the word of God is living and powerful, and sharper than any two-edged sword, piercing even to the division of soul and spirit, and of joints and marrow, and is a discerner of the thoughts and intents of the heart; And there is no creature hidden from His sight, but all things are naked and open to the eyes of Him to whom we must give account.

Hebrews 4:12-13

REMOVE A CURSE

Prepare a purple candle to repel.

Now to the King eternal, immortal, invisible, to God who alone is wise, be honor and glory forever and ever, Amen.

1 Timothy 1:17

MAKE GOOD WISHES COME TRUE

Prepare a red candle to attract.

Many, O LORD my God, are Your wonderful works Which You have done; And Your thoughts toward us Cannot be recounted to You in order; If I would declare and speak of them, They are more than can be numbered.

Psalms 40:5

BRING BACK A LOST LOVER

Prepare a pink candle to attract.

Ask, and it will be given to you; seek, and you will find; knock, and it will be opened to you. For everyone who asks receives, and the one who seeks finds, and to the one who knocks it will be opened.

Matthew 7:7-8

TO REMOVE THE EVIL EYE

Prepare a white candle to repel.

And it is God who establishes us with you in Christ, and has anointed us, and who has also put his seal on us and given us his Spirit in our hearts as a guarantee.

2 Corinthians 1:21-22

HELP A FRIEND WHO IS DEPRESSED

Prepare a blue candle to attract.

Do not love the world or the things in the world. If anyone loves the world, the love of the Father is not in him. For all that is in the world—the desires of the flesh and the desires of the eyes and pride in possessions—is not from the Father but is from the world. And the world is passing away along with its desires, but whoever does the will of God abides forever.

1 John 2:15-17

Forbidden Magic Spells From The Bible

TO GAIN SPIRITUAL POWER

Prepare a purple candle to attract.

And they did bind the breastplate by his rings unto the rings of the ephod with a lace of blue, that it might be above the curious girdle of the ephod, and that the breastplate might not be loosed from the ephod; as the Lord commanded Moses.

Exodus 39:21

TO OVERCOME A STRONG ENEMY

Prepare a purple candle to repel.

And now thou sayest, Go, tell thy lord, Behold, Elijah is here.

1 Kings 18:11

TO MAKE GOOD FRIENDS

Prepare a red candle to attract.

Again, think ye that we excuse ourselves unto you? We speak before God in Christ: but we do all things, dearly beloved, for your edifying.

2 Corinthians 12:19

END AN ARGUMENT

Prepare a purple candle to repel.

And set up false witnesses, which said, This man ceaseth not to speak blasphemous words against this holy place, and the law.

Acts 6:13

GAIN FORGIVENESS

Prepare a blue candle to attract.

And he said unto them, I am an Hebrew; and I fear the Lord, the God of heaven, which hath made the sea and the dry land.

Jonah 1:9

FOR RECONCILIATION

Prepare a blue candle to attract.

And I will set the Egyptians against the Egyptians: and they shall fight every one against his brother, and every one against his neighbor; city against city, and kingdom against kingdom.

Isaiah 19:2

MAKE SOMEONE DREAM OF YOU

Prepare a white candle to attract.

My soul hath kept thy testimonies; and I love them exceedingly.

Psalms 119:167

TO TURN AN ENEMY INTO A FRIEND

Prepare a purple candle to attract.

A time to cast away stones, and a time to gather stones together; a time to embrace, and a time to refrain from embracing.

Ecclesiastes 3:5

CLEANSE A HOME FROM NEGATIVE ENERGY

Prepare a white candle to repel.

That it might be fulfilled which was spoken by the prophet, saying, I will open my mouth in parables; I will utter things which have been kept secret from the foundation of the world.

Matthew 13:35

RID HOME OF TROUBLESOME SPIRITS

Prepare white candle to repel.

And that which thou sowest, thou sowest not that body that shall be, but bare grain, it may chance of wheat, or of some other grain.

1 Corinthians 15:37

ENHANCE YOUR POWERS PHYSICALLY AND MENTALLY

Prepare a red candle to attract.

And I will encamp about mine house because of the army, because of him that passeth by, and because of him that returneth: and no oppressor shall pass through them any more: for now have I seen with mine eyes.

Zechariah 9:8

TO GAIN INNER STRENGTH

Prepare a blue candle to attract.

But grow in grace, and in the knowledge of our Lord and Saviour Jesus Christ. To him be glory both now and for ever. Amen.

2 Peter 3:18

FOR WISDOM AND KNOWLEDGE

Prepare a green candle to attract.

Every valley shall be filled, and every mountain and hill shall be brought low; and the crooked shall be made straight, and the rough ways shall be made smooth.

Luke 3:5

TO LOSE YOUR TROUBLES

Prepare a blue candle to repel.

And Pharaoh said unto him, Get thee from me, take heed to thyself, see my face no more; for in that day thou seest my face thou shalt die.

Exodus 10:28

REMOVE BAD LUCK AND ALL CURSES

Prepare a white candle to repel.

Nevertheless they were disobedient, and rebelled against thee, and cast thy law behind their backs, and slew thy prophets which testified against them to turn them to thee, and they wrought great provocations.

Nehemiah 9:26

TO RECEIVE AN ANSWER TO A QUESTION

Prepare a blue candle to attract.

Woe is me! for I am as when they have gathered the summer fruits, as the grapegleanings of the vintage: there is no cluster to eat: my soul desired the firstripe fruit.

Micah 7:1

TO GET A BETTER JOB

Prepare a green candle to attract.

For the Lamb which is in the midst of the throne shall feed them, and shall lead them unto living fountains of waters: and God shall wipe away all tears from their eyes.

Revelation 7:17

FOR SUCCESS IN BUSINESS

Prepare a green candle to attract.

They shall be abundantly satisfied with the fatness of thy house; and thou shalt make them drink of the river of thy pleasures.

Psalms 36:8

RID YOURSELF OF TROUBLES WITH MONEY OR BUSINESS

Prepare a green candle to repel.

I will also make it a possession for the bittern, and pools of water: and I will sweep it with the besom of destruction, saith the LORD of hosts.

Isaiah 14:23

STOP YOUR BOSS FROM BOTHERING YOU

Prepare a purple candle to repel.

Yet will I leave a remnant, that ye may have some that shall escape the sword among the nations, when ye shall be scattered through the countries.

Ezekiel 6:8

TO GET BETTER WORK FROM EMPLOYEES

Prepare a purple candle to attract.

Lord, my heart is not haughty, nor mine eyes lofty: neither do I exercise myself in great matters, or in things too high for me.

Psalms 131:1

RISE ABOVE ANY COMPETITION

Prepare a red candle to attract.

A wise king scattereth the wicked, and bringeth the wheel over them.

Proverbs 20:26

SUCCESS FROM UNFAIR COMPETITION

Prepare a red candle to repel.

The wrath of God came upon them, and slew the fattest of them, and smote down the chosen men of Israel.

Psalms 78:31

TO ATTRACT CUSTOMERS

Prepare a green candle to attract.

And the multitudes gave heed with one accord unto the things that were spoken by Philip, when they heard, and saw the signs which he did.

Acts 8:6

TO RID YOURSELF OF BAD DREAMS

Prepare a white candle to repel.

and those that weep, as though they wept not; and those that rejoice, as though they rejoiced not; and those that buy, as though they possessed not;

1 Corinthians 7:30

TO RID SOMEONE ELSE OF BAD DREAMS

Prepare a white candle to repel.

My heart fluttereth, horror hath affrighted me; the twilight that I desired hath been turned into trembling unto me.

Isaiah 21:4

TO HAVE A NIGHT OF PLEASANT DREAMS

Prepare a white candle to attract.

And I will lay thy flesh upon the mountains, and fill the valleys with thy height.

Ezekiel 32:5

TO HAVE A TROUBLE FREE NIGHT OF SLEEP

Prepare a white candle to attract.

And when the dew that lay was gone up, behold, upon the face of the wilderness a small round thing, small as the hoar-frost on the ground.

Exodus 16:14

ALWAYS AWAKEN FRESH AND FULL OF ENERGY

Prepare a red candle to attract.

And so it was, when the cloud abode from even unto the morning, and that the cloud was taken up in the morning, then they journeyed: whether it was by day or by night that the cloud was taken up, they journeyed.

Numbers 9:21

STOP A LOVER FROM CHEATING

Prepare a pink candle to attract.

through whom also we have had our access by faith into this grace wherein we stand; and we rejoice in hope of the glory of God.

Romans 5:2

STOP SOMEONE FROM STEALING YOUR LOVER

Prepare a pink candle to repel.

When I say unto the wicked, Thou shalt surely die; and thou givest him not warning, nor speakest to warn the wicked from his wicked way, to save his life; the same wicked man shall die in his iniquity; but his blood will I require at thy hand.

Ezekiel 3:18

REKINDLE THE FIRE IN A ROMANCE

Prepare a red candle to attract.

For to do whatsoever thy hand and thy counsel determined before to be done.

Acts 4:28

Forbidden Magic Spells From The Bible

TO BE A BETTER LOVER

Prepare a red candle to attract.

And call upon me in the day of trouble; I will deliver thee, and thou shalt glorify me.

Psalms 50:15

TO HAVE YOUR PARTNER BE A BETTER LOVER

Prepare a red candle to attract.

He brought me forth also into a large place; He delivered me, because he delighted in me.

Psalms 18:19

FIND A BETTER LOVER

Prepare a red candle to attract.

For this is he, of whom it is written, Behold, I send my messenger before thy face, which shall prepare thy way before thee.

Matthew 11:10

CONTACT YOUR GUARDIAN ANGEL

Prepare a purple candle to attract.

They are of the world: therefore speak they of the world, and the world heareth them.

1 John 4:5

CONTACT AN ASCENDED MASTER

Prepare a white candle to attract.

For he shall never be moved; The righteous shall be had in everlasting remembrance.

Psalms 112:6

CONTACT YOUR SPIRIT GUIDE

Prepare a purple candle to attract.

Whom I have sent unto you for the same purpose, that ye might know our affairs, and that he might comfort your hearts.

Ephesians 6:22

PROTECTION FROM MALEVOLENT SPIRITS

Prepare a purple candle to repel.

From above hath he sent fire into my bones, and it prevaileth against them: he hath spread a net for my feet, he hath turned me back: he hath made me desolate and faint all the day.

Lamentations 1:13

TO HELP A TROUBLED SOUL FIND PEACE

Prepare a pink candle to attract.

From above hath he sent fire into my bones, and it prevaileth against them: he hath spread a net for my feet, he hath turned me back: he hath made me desolate and faint all the day.

Lamentations 1:13

TO GAIN PROSPECTIVE IN THE FACE OF DIFFICULTY

Prepare a blue candle to attract.

Now therefore, our God, the great, the mighty, and the terrible God, who keepest covenant and loving kindness, let not all the travail seem little before thee, that hath come upon us, on our kings, on our princes, and on our priests, and on our prophets, and on our fathers, and on all people, since the time of the kings of Assyria unto this day.

Nehemiah 9:32

TO BRING JOY AND HAPPINESS TO YOUR FAMILY

Prepare a green candle to attract.

I communed with mine own heart, saying, Lo, I have gotten me great wisdom above all that were before me in Jerusalem; yea, my heart hath had great experience of wisdom and knowledge.

Ecclesiastes 1:16

TO DISPEL FEAR

Prepare a purple candle to repel.

He mocketh at fear, and is not affrighted; neither turneth he back from the sword.

Job 39:22

Forbidden Magic Spells From The Bible

VI. Sacred Stones

CRYSTALS and gemstones have played an important role in mankind's mystical development. From the beginning of time, early man was drawn to the beautiful stones that glistened and glittered in the sun. But besides the obvious beauty of crystals and gemstones, people soon realized that these stones carried within them a power that was beyond explanation.

Archaeologists have discovered in graves and barrows excavated in Europe, the Middle East, Russia, and Africa, beads, carvings, and jewelry of amber, jet, turquoise, lapis, garnet, carnelian, quartz and other stones. It is believed that the carvings were probably amulets and talismans used for protection and as reminders of religious rites.

Some of the discovered stones were carved in the shape of various animals, and were probably symbols of particular totems. Others were necklaces and other items of adornment. The value given to crystals in these various cultures is indicated by their presence in the graves; they were intended to go with the departed soul to help them in the next life.

In ancient Egypt, crystal was widely used and a hieroglyphic papyrus from the year 2000 B.C.E. documents a medical cure using a crystal. Lapis was considered to be a royal stone and it was often crushed and made into a poultice to be rubbed into the crown of the head. It was believed that as it dried it drew out all spiritual impurities.

The pharaohs often had their headdresses lined with malachite in the belief that it helped them to rule wisely. In powder form this stone was used for poor eyesight and inner vision. Many other stones were found in Egyptian tombs, including carnelian, turquoise, and tiger's eye. These were often shaped into amulets, shields, and into the shapes of hearts, the Eye of Horus and scarabs.

Forbidden Magic Spells From The Bible

Crystals and gemstones also played an important role in ancient India. Teachings about the body's energy centers called chakras and their relationship with crystals for meditation originated from India. Astrological documents written as early as 400 B.C.E. contain detailed observations about the power of various stones to counteract the negative effects of planetary positions.

Gemstones were regarded as having great spiritual and emotional powers. Moonstone, for instance, was a sacred stone, and believed to arouse love. Onyx, in contrast, was believed to help release the ties of old loves. The ruby was a highly valued gemstone, and was known as the "King of Precious Stones."

The connection between humans and crystals is especially vibrant in the following verses from the Hindu sacred texts Vedas:

There is an endless net of threads

Throughout the universe.

The horizontal threads are in space.

The vertical threads are in time.

At every crossing of the threads,

There is an individual,

And every individual

Is a crystal bead.

The great light of absolute being

Illuminates and penetrates

Every crystal bead, and also,

Every crystal bead reflects

Not only the light

From every other crystal in the net,

But also every reflection

Of every reflection

Throughout the universe.

Forbidden Magic Spells From The Bible

SACRED STONES IN THE BIBLE

The use of crystals and sacred stones for mystical purposes was common among the peoples of the Holy lands. Called amulets, these magical charms were made in the form of small pendants attached to a necklace or bracelet. They were worn to protect a person from negative energies, evil and injury, and also to bring good luck.

In the Old Testament there were twelve sacred gemstones that came from the Mountain of God, where Moses received the Ten Commandments. They were given to Moses, whose blueprint for a sacred breastplate for his brother, the high priest Aaron, is given in Exodus, 28:15-21:

> *And thou shalt make the rational of judgment with embroidered work of divers colors, according to the workmanship of the ephod, of gold, violet, and purple, and scarlet twice dyed, and fine twisted linen. It shall be four square and doubled: it shall be the measure of a span both in length and in breadth. And thou shalt set in it four rows of stones. In the first row shall be a sardius stone, and a topaz, and an emerald: In the second a carbuncle, a sapphire, and a jasper: In the third a ligurius, an agate, and an amethyst: In the fourth a chrysolite, an onyx, and a beryl. They shall be set in gold by their rows. And they shall have the names of the children of Israel: with twelve names shall they be engraved, each stone with the name of one according to the twelve tribes.*

The Jewish Encyclopedia says that the vestments of the high priest were interpreted in three ways. The explanation of Philo is as follows ("Vita Mosis," iii. 209): His upper garment was the symbol of the ether, while the blossoms represented the earth, the pomegranates typified running water, and the bells denoted the music of the water. The ephod corresponded to heaven, and the stones on both shoulders to the two hemispheres, one above and the other below the earth. The six names on each of the stones were the six signs of the zodiac, which were denoted also by the twelve names on the breastplate. The miter was the sign of the crown which exalted the high priest above all earthly kings.

Josephus' explanation is this: The coat was the symbol of the earth, the upper garment emblemized heaven, while the bells and pomegranates represented thunder and lightning. The ephod typified the four elements, and

73

the interwoven gold denoted the glory of God. The breastplate was in the center of the ephod, as the earth formed the center of the universe; the girdle symbolized the ocean, the stones on the shoulders the sun and moon, and the jewels in the breastplate the twelve signs of the zodiac, while the miter was a token of heaven.

Many of these same gemstones are listed in Ezekiel, Chapter 28 in reference to the King of Tyrus. Said to have the power to summon angels; the book of Ezekiel, Chapter 28:13-16, calls them "The Stones of Fire."

There is the mention of the use of two onyx stones, along with 12 stones in the breastplate, and the mention of two very mysterious stones called the Urim and Thummim which were used to divine the will of God. These two mysterious stones are kept within the breastplate, and so the breastplate is called the "breastplate of judgment."

There are also twelve gemstones listed in Revelation, Chapter 21. These sacred gemstones are: Jasper, Sapphire, Chalcedony, Emerald, Sardonyx, Sardius, Chrysolite, Beryl, Topaz, Chrysoprasus, Jacinth, and Amethyst.

Many scholars believe that the gems are the same twelve "Stones of Fire," that were in Aaron's Breast Plate of Judgment. In St. John the Divine's vision of the Heavenly Jerusalem, the City stood on a foundation of 12 stones, each correlating with one of the stones of the breast plate. The stones, though, are in a different order – with the last stone of the breastplate (the stone associated with the tribe of Benjamin) listed first.

According to some, the literal reason for these vestments was that they denoted the disposition of the terrestrial globe; as though the high-priest confessed himself to be the minister of the Creator of the world, wherefore it is written (Wis. 18:24): "In the robe" of Aaron "was the whole world" described. For the linen breeches signified the earth out of which the flax grows.

The surrounding belt signified the ocean which surrounds the earth. The violet tunic denoted the air by its color: its little bells betoken the thunder; the pomegranates, the lightning. The ephod, by its many colors, signified the starry heaven; the two onyx stones denoted the two hemispheres, or the sun and moon.

The twelve precious stones on the breast are the twelve signs of the zodiac: and they are said to have been placed on the rational because in heaven, are the types of earthly things, according to Job 38:33: "Dost thou know the order of heaven, and canst thou set down the reason thereof on the earth?" The turban or tiara signified the empyrean: the golden plate was a token of God, the governor of the universe.

In the 1913 book *The Curious Lore of Precious Stones*, author George F. Kunz recounts the early beliefs of Andreas, bishop of Caesurae, who lived in the last half of the 10th century C.E. Andreas was one of the first to associate with the Apostles of Jesus the symbolism of the 12 gemstones.

The Jasper, which like the emerald is of a greenish hue, signifies St. Peter.

The Sapphire is likened to the Heavens (from this stone is made a color popularly called lazur) and signifies St. Paul.

The Chalcedony may well have been considered what we now call the carbuncle and represented St. Andrew.

The Emerald, which is of a green color, is nourished with oil that its transparency and beauty may not change; this stone signifies St. John the Evangelist.

The Sardonyx, which shows a certain transparency and purity of the human nail, represents James.

The Sardius with its tawny and translucent coloring suggests fire and represents Philip.

The Chrysolite, gleaming with the splendor of gold, symbolizes Bartholomew.

The Beryl, imitating the colors of the sea and air, and not unlike the jacinth, suggests Thomas.

The Topaz, which is of a ruddy color, resembling somewhat the carbuncle, denotes Matthew.

The Chrysoprase, more brightly tinged with a gold hue than gold itself, symbolizes St. Thaddaeus.

The Jacinth, which is of a celestial hue, signifies Simon.

The Amethyst, which shows to the onlooker a fiery aspect, signifies Matthew.

On pages 289-301 of Kunz's book, there is information concerning the ancient names of the stones and what they are named today. In the following list, the ancient or biblical name is given, followed by the modern name in parentheses. They are: Sardius (Carnelian), Topaz (Peridot), Chalcedony (Emerald), Emerald (Almandine garnet), Sapphire (Lapis Lazuli), Sardonyx (Onyx), Jacinth (Agate), Amethystos (Amethyst), Chrysoprase (Citrine), Agate(Agate), Jasper (Jasper), and Onyx (Turquoise).

The last item to consider about the 12 stones is the significance of color. The colors or patterns are, as recounted by Andreas: green, blue, red, translucent tan, orange, golden, sky blue, purple.

The colors of the stones have their own Christian symbolic meaning:

Green: Canonical color for use on Sunday. Hope, joy, and the bright promises of youth.

Blue and Sky Blue: An emblem of the Celestial regions and Celestial virtues. In Christian art, the Virgin, Saints, and Angels are often depicted in blue robes.

Red: This color is used in ceremonies concerned with the Pentecost, and at various religious feasts. It suggests and symbolizes suffering and martyrdom for the faith, and the supreme sacrifice of Christ upon the Cross. Divine love and majesty are also typified by this color.

Dull yellow or tan: The color has a connotation of treachery and envy. Hence Judas was dressed in dull yellow or tan clothing. Heretics were required to wear clothing of this hue when they were condemned to the stake in medieval times.

Orange and golden yellow: This color is emblematic of God's goodness and of faith and good works. The color of the sun from the beginning of man's recognition of things spiritual has had major significance.

Violet: A canonical color which is appropriate for use during Lent, and on Advent Sunday, along with Septuagesima and Quinquagesima Sundays. The chastening and purifying effects of suffering find expression in this color.

THE POWER OF CRYSTALS AND GEMSTONES

Even though it is not listed as one of the 12 stones, crystal was an important gemstone in the Holy land. In the Bible, crystal was referred to under a number of different names. Hebrew **ghbsh** (Job 28:18), **qrh** (Ezekiel 1:22): both words signify a glassy substance; Septuagint gabis; Vulgate eminentia (Job 28:18); **krystallos, crystallus** (Ezekiel 1:22). — This was a transparent mineral resembling glass, most probably a variety of quartz. Job places it in the same category with gold, onyx, sapphire, glass, coral, topaz, etc. The Targum renders the **qrt** of Ezech. by "ice"; the versions translate by "crystal."

Crystals and gemstones can hold and convey power, spiritual energy; they can amplify and serve as vehicles of energy, and can be vehicles of spiritual energy, Divine Power. This is especially true of gemstones and crystals, the expression of the highest of life in the mineral realm.

All gemstones and crystals have a capacity to hold and convey spiritual energy, but among any kind of gemstone or crystal are those that have a very special or extraordinary capacity to do so – it is as though they are blessed or "charmed," as though they were specifically destined for sacred use, spiritual work; these are the stones we seek and use in our art of divine theurgy or wonderworking.

Among crystals there are different forms, different shapes, different kinds – and they may be used for different theurgic operations, different divine works. A "generator" does exactly what the term implies – it generates a field of energy-intelligence or light-power extending into the space around it; it is a whole natural crystal, usually cut at its base, which stands upright freely, usually of some size and substance. In Sophian teachings these are called "great stones," "key stones," "cornerstones" or "earth-keepers," and larger ones have also been called "archangelic stones,"

When we invoke light-power, the divine powers, in a theurgic working, these stones serve as material talismans of the spiritual energy – they become a physical vehicle and matrix of the divine force invoked, as though an interface between the spiritual energy and the material dimension.

The direct influx of the divine powers can be too intense and overwhelming for many individuals; in terms of the Creative Force, there are relatively few individuals who can receive the direct influx and not become swiftly overwhelmed. Crystals, however, can be used like power transformers, serving to downgrade the influx of Divine Power, making it accessible to more individuals.

Experiencing and receiving something of the Divine Power at a lower grade, of course, can serve to upgrade a person's energy and soul, and thus facilitate the experience and reception of Divine Power at a higher grade – in other words the use of crystals is skillful means, a help along the way, as with many tools we use, even the spiritual practices themselves.

This was the very purpose of the stones used in the outfit of the high priest – an interface of the Divine Power with the material dimension and a downgrading of the Divine Power making it accessible at a lower level. According to the Holy Torah, the Divine Power flowing from the ark of covenant was so intense that even if the most righteous person touched it, with good intention, they would fall dead. So, indeed, whatever the Divine Power that was moving among them, there was a need to bring it down to a material level when communicating to the people.

In the Kabbalah the knowledge and wisdom of the use of sacred stones and sacred places in the earth corresponds to Archangels Uriel and Sandalfon, and to the Divine Name of Adonai – it is part of the wisdom of Malkut, the Shekinah display of Malkut of Malkut.

PREPARING A CRYSTAL

When it comes to using crystals or gemstones, personal preference on what type of stone to use is generally the best course to follow. Most people do not have a wide range of different types of gemstones to choose from before attempting a magic spell. Because of this I have picked Bible-based spells that can be best used with quartz crystals, the most common type of crystal used by practitioners.

By no means does this suggest that you cannot use these spells with other types and colors of gemstones. Again, personal preference is the key here. You may find that your personal energies resonate best with a moonstone, or a piece of pink tourmaline, so feel free to experiment with a wide variety of stones if you have them at your disposal.

The practitioner can try one of the 12 sacred stones of fire from the Bible, or a gemstone that is one of the sacred colors. Consult the list in chapter two for other types of crystals and gemstones and their attributes. Whatever type of gemstone you decide to use, always make sure that your stone has been "cleared" before using it.

Clearing has to do with the energy of the stone or crystal. Crystals can be charged with our thought vibrations and then act on our subtle energy fields. When used with Bible-based magic, they help to create situations in our lives that will lead us in directions that allow positive growth and healing. Clearing a crystal or gemstone is a simple task, and it is a way to insure that there are no left over energies from a previous spell. It is a way to reprogram your crystal, and create a new energy bond for each and every spell.

There are many ways to do this, but this is a simple and effective way; first, make sure you will not be disturbed. Next, hold your crystal under running water, and as the water pours over it, close your eyes and imagine all the negative energies are washed away down the drain and out to the vast ocean to be purified by the cycles of life. You can also leave your stone in the warm sun, and allow the power of light to purify the crystal. Another excellent method is to burn a little sage and pass your gemstone several times through the smoke

To charge your new crystal for a new Bible verse spell, you are encouraging or awaking the stone to help you or someone else with the properties it possess. By charging, you are asking for a specific kind of help and you let the stone know which powers you need.

Charging is simply done by holding the stones in your projective hand (right if right handed - left if left handed), visualizing your magical need, and pouring energy out from your body into the stone. Once you can feel the vibrations—you know that the stone has been charged. As with any Bible-based spell, before you begin make sure that you have some time to yourself where you will not be disturbed by any sort of distractions. Take the phone off the hook and lock yourself away in a quiet room with the lights turned down. If you desire, you can play a little soft music to enhance the mood.

Sit quietly for a while and concentrate on what it is that you want your spell to accomplish. Hold your crystal in your hands and try to visualize the energies of your desire combining and resonating with the energies of your stone. If it helps with visualizing your desire, write down on a clean piece of white paper what you want to achieve.

When you are ready, say the Bible verse once out loud. For added power, repeat two more times for a total of three times. Afterwards, sit quietly for a few more minutes thinking about your desire and what you want to accomplish with it.

If you feel that your spell has been successful, that is all you have to do. If, however, it feels incomplete, you can repeat the same spell with the same crystal for six more days, a total of seven. If after three week have passed and you still have not received an answer to your spell, consider that the Universe may have other plans for you and a spell would be interfering with that fate. Wait about a month and try again if you so desire. Or you may want to change the wording of your desire to clarify what exactly you want to happen.

Take your paper and pen and write down what your fears are. Write about your anger, helplessness, and the craziness of your life, or in the lives of those you wish to protect. Write down every word of how you feel about the situation(s). Feel the stone taking on those things which frighten you or on those things that you wish to have protected. When you are through, hold the crystal and let its energies overwhelm you and feel its strength making you stronger.

CRYSTAL SPELL TO INCREASE LOVE BETWEEN

A COUPLE

Suggested gemstone: rose quartz

Finally, brethren, whatsoever things are true, whatsoever things are honorable, whatsoever things are just, whatsoever things are pure, whatsoever things are lovely, whatsoever things are of good report; if there be any virtue, and if there be any praise, think on these things.

Philippians 4:8

CRYSTAL SPELL FOR NEW ROMANCE

Suggested gemstone: alexandrite

It was but a little that I passed from them, When I found him whom my soul loveth: I held him, and would not let him go, Until I had brought him into my mother's house, And into the chamber of her that conceived me.

The Song of Solomon 3:4

Forbidden Magic Spells From The Bible

CRYSTAL SPELL TO HAVE SOMEONE NOTICE YOU

Suggested gemstone: calcite

So that thou incline thine ear unto wisdom, and apply thine heart to understanding;

Proverbs 2:2

CRYSTAL SPELL FOR RECONCILIATION

Suggested gemstone: sapphire

I love them that love me; and those that seek me early shall find me.

Proverbs 8:17

CRYSTAL SPELL TO GET BACK A LOVER WHO IS WITH SOMEONE ELSE

Suggested gemstone: agate

Therefore shall ye lay up these my words in your heart and in your soul; and ye shall bind them for a sign upon your hand, and they shall be for frontlets between your eyes.

Deuteronomy 11:18

CRYSTAL SPELL TO REMOVE NEGATIVE FEELINGS FROM YOUR HEART

Suggested gemstone: topaz

Depart not hence, I pray thee, until I come unto thee, and bring forth my present, and set it before thee. And he said, I will tarry until thou come again.

Judges 6:18

CRYSTAL SPELL TO GET OUT OF A BAD SITUATION

Suggested gemstone: carnelian

Our soul is escaped as a bird out of the snare of the fowlers: the snare is broken, and we are escaped.

Psalms 124:7

CRYSTAL SPELL TO BRING HOPE AND COMFORT

Suggested gemstone: hematite

For thou didst cast me into the depth, in the heart of the seas, And the flood was round about me; All thy waves and thy billows passed over me.

Jonah 2:3

CRYSTAL SPELL TO EASE THE HEART

Suggested gemstone: calcite

And it shall come to pass, when many evils and troubles are come upon them, that this song shall testify before them as a witness; for it shall not be forgotten out of the mouths of their seed: for I know their imagination which they frame this day, before I have brought them into the land which I sware.

Deuteronomy 31:21

CRYSTAL SPELL TO FIND JOY

Suggested gemstone: amethyst

But they that escape of them shall escape, and shall be on the mountains like doves of the valleys, all of them mourning, every one for his iniquity.

Ezekiel 7:16

Forbidden Magic Spells From The Bible

CRYSTAL SPELL TO KEEP BAD LUCK AT BAY

Suggested gemstone: cat's-eye

The LORD is my shepherd; I shall not want.

Psalms 23:1

CRYSTAL SPELL TO REMOVE EVIL EYE

Suggested gemstone: moonstone

But let him that glorieth glory in this, that he understandeth and knoweth me, that I am the Lord which exercise loving kindness, judgment, and righteousness, in the earth: for in these things I delight, saith the Lord.

Jeremiah 9:24

CRYSTAL SPELL TO REMOVE CURSES

Suggested gemstone: opal

My tongue also shall talk of thy righteousness all the day long; For they are put to shame, for they are confounded, that seek my hurt.

Psalms 71:24

CRYSTAL SPELL TO TURN ENEMIES INTO FRIENDS

Suggested gemstone: turquoise

And ye shall chase your enemies, and they shall fall before you by the sword.

Leviticus 26:7

CRYSTAL SPELL TO PREVENT ATTACK AND THIEVES

Suggested gemstone: chrysoprase

If a soul sin, and commit a trespass against the LORD, and lie unto his neighbor in that which was delivered him to keep, or in fellowship, or in a thing taken away by violence, or hath deceived his neighbor;

Leviticus 6:2

CRYSTAL SPELL TO STOP LIES AND DECEIT

Suggested gemstone: sardonyx

The Lord judge between me and thee, and the Lord avenge me of thee: but mine hand shall not be upon thee.

1 Samuel 24:12

CRYSTAL SPELL TO REGAIN PEACE AFTER AN ARGUMENT

Suggested gemstone: sunstone

I have trodden the winepress alone; and of the people there was none with me: for I will tread them in mine anger, and trample them in my fury; and their blood shall be sprinkled upon my garments, and I will stain all my raiment.

Isaiah 63:3

CRYSTAL SPELL TO STOP PERSECUTION FROM KNOWN AND SECRET ENEMIES

Suggested gemstone: peridot

All that found them have devoured them; and their adversaries said, We are not guilty, because they have sinned against Jehovah, the habitation of righteousness, even Jehovah, the hope of their fathers. - Jeremiah 50:7

Forbidden Magic Spells From The Bible

CRYSTAL SPELL TO FIGHT OFF PSYCHIC ATTACK

Suggested gemstone: obsidian

Oh that thou wouldest rend the heavens, that thou wouldest come down, that the mountains might quake at thy presence.

Isaiah 64:1

CRYSTAL SPELL FOR SAFETY

Suggested gemstone: lepidolite

But we were gentle in the midst of you, as when a nurse

cherisheth her own children.

1 Thessalonians 2:7

CRYSTAL SPELL TO REMOVE A BINDING SPELL

Suggested gemstone: malachite

Because of his strength I will give heed unto thee; For God is

my high tower.

Psalms 59:9

CRYSTAL SPELL TO PROTECT ALL LOVED ONES

Suggested gemstone: amethyst

But God shall wound the head of his enemies, and the hairy scalp of such an one as goeth on still in his trespasses.

Psalms 68:21

Forbidden Magic Spells From The Bible

CRYSTAL SPELL FOR GOOD LUCK

Suggested gemstone: apache tear

Sing unto Jehovah a new song, and his praise from the end of the earth; ye that go down to the sea, and all that is therein, the isles, and the inhabitants thereof.

Isaiah 42:10

CRYSTAL SPELL FOR SEVEN DAYS OF GOOD LUCK

Suggested gemstone: staurolite

Yea, thou doest away with fear, And hinderest devotion before God.

Job 15:4

CRYSTAL SPELL TO CHANGE YOUR LUCK

Suggested gemstone: green aventurine

And on my behalf, that utterance may be given unto me in opening my mouth, to make known with boldness the mystery of the gospel.

Ephesians 6:19

CRYSTAL SPELL TO FIND SOMETHING THAT WAS LOST

Suggested gemstone: agate

For he bringeth down them that dwell on high; the lofty city, he layeth it low; he layeth it low, even to the ground; he bringeth it even to the dust.

Isaiah 26:5

Forbidden Magic Spells From The Bible

CRYSTAL SPELL TO OVERCOME SHYNESS

Suggested gemstone: tourmaline

Behold now, I have opened my mouth; My tongue hath spoken in my mouth.

Job 33:2

CRYSTAL SPELL FOR CLARITY OF THOUGHT

Suggested gemstone: chrysocolla

And now, behold, the hand of the Lord is upon thee, and thou shalt be blind, not seeing the sun for a season. And immediately there fell on him a mist and a darkness; and he went about seeking some to lead him by the hand.

Acts 13:11

CRYSTAL SPELL TO SEE THE FUTURE IN DREAMS

Suggested gemstone: amazonite

In a dream, in a vision of the night, When deep sleep falleth upon men, In slumberings upon the bed;

Job 33:15

CRYSTAL SPELL TO GAIN GREAT HONOR

Suggested gemstone: labradorite

If a man therefore purge himself from these, he shall be a vessel unto honour, sanctified, and meet for the master's use, and prepared unto every good work.

2 Timothy 2:21

Forbidden Magic Spells From The Bible

CRYSTAL SPELL TO GET RID OF EVIL SPIRITS

Suggested gemstone: bloodstone

And Jesus rebuked him, saying, Hold thy peace, and come out of him. And when the devil had thrown him in the midst, he came out of him, and hurt him not.

Luke 4:35

CRYSTAL SPELL TO RESIST TEMPTATION

Suggested gemstone: pietersite

Enter not into the path of the wicked, and go not in the way of evil men.

Proverbs 4:14

CRYSTAL SPELL FOR PERSONAL PROTECTION

Suggested gemstone: staurolite

For thou hast been a refuge for me, A strong tower from the enemy.

Psalms 61:3

CRYSTAL SPELL FOR SUCCESS IN THE LOTTERY

Suggested gemstone: sapphire

And take double money in your hand; and the money that was brought again in the mouth of your sacks, carry it again in your hand; peradventure it was an oversight:

Genesis 43:12

Forbidden Magic Spells From The Bible

CRYSTAL SPELL FOR WEALTH AND PROSPERITY

Suggested gemstone: citrine

Bring ye all the tithes into the storehouse, that there may be meat in mine house, and prove me now herewith, saith the Lord of hosts, if I will not open you the windows of heaven, and pour you out a blessing, that there shall not be room enough to receive it.

Malachi 3:10

CRYSTAL SPELL TO BANISH DEBT

Suggested gemstone: iolite (also known as cordierite)

He that receiveth a prophet in the name of a prophet shall receive a prophet's reward: and he that receiveth a righteous man in the name of a righteous man shall receive a righteous man's reward.

Matthew 10:41

CRYSTAL SPELL FOR SUCCESS WITHOUT HURTING OTHERS

Suggested gemstone: malachite

He that hath knowledge spareth his words: and a man of understanding is of an excellent spirit.

Proverbs 17:27

CRYSTAL SPELL TO BE MORE RESPONSIBLE WITH MONEY

Suggested gemstone: aventurine

The Lord of hosts hath sworn, saying, Surely as I have thought, so shall it come to pass; and as I have purposed, so shall it stand:

Isaiah 14:24

CRYSTAL SPELL TO LOOK BEYOND MATERIAL POSSESSIONS

Suggested gemstone: ametrine

Lay not up for yourselves treasures upon the earth, where moth and rust consume, and where thieves break through and steal:

Matthew 6:19

CRYSTAL SPELL FOR GREATER SPIRITUAL UNDERSTANDING

Suggested gemstone: amethyst

And it shall come to pass in the last days, saith God, I will pour out of my Spirit upon all flesh: and your sons and your daughters shall prophesy, and your young men shall see visions, and your old men shall dream dreams:

Acts 2:17

CRYSTAL SPELL TO OPEN YOUR THIRD EYE

Suggested gemstone: sodalite

Even the mystery which hath been hid from ages and from generations, but now is made manifest to his saints:

Colossians 1:26

CRYSTAL SPELL TO SEE THE TRUTH

Suggested gemstone: azurite

And art confident that thou thyself art a guide of the blind, a light of them which are in darkness,

Romans 2:19

Forbidden Magic Spells From The Bible

CRYSTAL SPELL TO KNOW YOUR GUARDIAN ANGEL

Suggested gemstone: celestite (also known as celestine)

And the angel that talked with me came again, and waked me, as a man that is wakened out of his sleep,

Zechariah 4:1

CRYSTAL SPELL TO INCREASE PSYCHIC POWERS

Suggested gemstone: sugilite

And the Lord shall guide thee continually, and satisfy thy soul in drought, and make fat thy bones: and thou shalt be like a watered garden, and like a spring of water, whose waters fail not.

Isaiah 58:11

CRYSTAL SPELL TO RECEIVE DIVINE GRACE, LOVE AND MERCY

Suggested gemstone: seraphinite

Let the heavens be glad, and let the earth rejoice: and let men say among the nations, The Lord reigneth.

1 Chronicles 16:31

CRYSTAL SPELL FOR GREATER WISDOM FROM GOD

Suggested gemstone: sapphire

For nothing is hid, that shall not be made manifest; nor anything secret, that shall not be known and come to light.

Luke 8:17

Forbidden Magic Spells From The Bible

CRYSTAL SPELL TO SEND GODS BLESSINGS TO SOMEONE ELSE

Suggested gemstone: citrine

But they that wait upon the Lord shall renew their strength; they shall mount up with wings as eagles; they shall run, and not be weary; and they shall walk, and not faint.

Isaiah 40:31

CRYSTAL SPELL TO HELP A FRIEND FIND PEACE

Suggested gemstone: jade

The Lord hear thee in the day of trouble; the name of the God of Jacob defend thee;

Psalms 20:1

CRYSTAL SPELL TO END A BAD SITUATION

Suggested gemstone: aventurine

Heap on wood, kindle the fire, consume the flesh, and spice it well, and let the bones be burned.

Ezekiel 24:10

CRYSTAL SPELL TO SEE THE TRUTH

Suggested gemstone: agate

Therefore speak I to them in parables; because seeing they see not, and hearing they hear not, neither do they understand.

Matthew 13:13

CRYSTAL SPELL TO BE TRULY HAPPY

Suggested gemstone: peridot

A man' belly shall be satisfied with the fruit of his mouth; and with the increase of his lips shall he be filled.

Proverbs 18:20

CRYSTAL SPELL TO KEEP AWAY THOSE WHO WOULD HURT YOU

Suggested gemstone: chrysoberyl (cat's eye)

For he shall be like the heath in the desert, and shall not see when good cometh; but shall inhabit the parched places in the wilderness, in a salt land and not inhabited.

Jeremiah 17:6

CRYSTAL SPELL TO HELP A FRIEND IN A BAD SITUATION

Suggested gemstone: amber

Wherefore let them that suffer according to the will of God commit the keeping of their souls to him in well doing, as unto a faithful Creator.

1 Peter 4:19

CRYSTAL SPELL TO END A SICKNESS

Suggested gemstone: quartz crystal

And the people, when they knew it, followed him: and he received them, and spake unto them of the kingdom of God, and healed them that had need of healing.

Luke 9:11

Forbidden Magic Spells From The Bible

CRYSTAL SPELL TO HEAL A FRIEND

Suggested gemstone: rhodonite

What is it then? I will pray with the spirit, and I will pray with the understanding also: I will sing with the spirit, and I will sing with the understanding also.

1 Corinthians 14:15

CRYSTAL SPELL TO HEAL YOUR AURA

Suggested gemstone: labradorite

It is the spirit that quickeneth: the flesh profiteth nothing. The words that I have spoken to you, are spirit and life.

John 6:63

CRYSTAL SPELL TO HEAL ALL WOUNDS

Suggested gemstone: red/banded agate

Therefore, thus says the Lord GOD, 'Because you have made your iniquity to be remembered, in that your transgressions are uncovered, so that in all your deeds your sins appear--because you have come to remembrance, you will be seized with the hand.

Ezekiel 21:24

VII. The Ancient Art of Incense Burning

SINCE ANCIENT times, incense has been burned as a deity offering, spiritual cleansing, mood setting, or for magical purposes. The Bible says in Exodus 30:1, "Thou shalt make an Altar to burn Incense on." History tells us that incense has been used as a sacrifice to the Deity, as a demonifuge to drive away evil spirits, and because people believe that it will bring good luck and enable them to gain their desires in love, money matters and other forms of magical workings.

Our mental state and emotions can be profoundly affected by scents and fragrances. They can stimulate, calm, and regularize. To calm reduce anxiety, stress, and fear, we use incense that has a direct and relaxing influence on the psyche.

Burn incense in the evening, while listening to soft background music and candlelight, relaxing as all your tensions and troubles dissipate along with the fragrant smoke. Incense can also have stimulating as well as revitalizing effects, and may be helpful in strengthening our potential and energy when we feel weak, discouraged, or exhausted.

The practice of burning incense to accompany invocations, prayers and spells is particularly favored by practitioners of Bible-based magic. In addition, if a Bible Verse spell involves a person far away, incense may be burned to "carry" the wish or desire to him or her. Incense if particularly good to help carry a spell across running water, which has a tendency to "carry" the energies of a spell away from who it was intended.

When incense is burned prior to magical workings, fragrant smoke also purifies the surrounding area of negative and disturbing vibrations. Though such purification is not usually necessary, it does help create the appropriate mental state necessary for the successful practice of magic. When the incense is smoldered in a ritual setting it undergoes a transformation. The vibrations, no longer trapped in their physical form, are released into the environment. Their energies, mixing with those who use them, speed out to effect the changes necessary to the manifestation of the magical goal.

The oldest and most original incenses used by mankind have been tree resins and herbs or woods that burn with a fragrant smoke. Typical herbal incenses include sage and tobacco, much favored by Native Americans and those who follow their traditions.

Sage is typically utilized in the form of wrapped and tied smudge sticks, while tobacco is burned in a ceremonial pipe. The best-known wood chip incense is the rare and expensive sandalwood, which is made of finely shaved chips of the tree of the same name. Resin incenses, which are granular lumps of dried tree sap, include the Biblical frankincense and myrrh as well as Benzoin and Copal, the latter a very special holy incense of the Mayan Indians of Central America.

Resins are often burned in mixtures, the light scent of golden frankincense combining beautifully with richly musky myrrh and sharply aromatic Benzoin. Another favorite mixture is cleansing camphor and purifying pine resin.

There are two types of incense that are used in magic: the combustible and the noncombustible. The former contains potassium nitrate (saltpeter) to aid in burning, while the latter does not. Therefore combustible incense can be burned in the form of bricks, cones, sticks and other shapes, whereas noncombustible incense must be sprinkled onto glowing charcoal blocks to release its fragrance.

USING INCENSE

Of all of the methods featured in this book, incense magic when used with Bible verses is probably the easiest to practice. The fragrant smoke from your incense actually does a lot of your work for you in settling your mind to focus on what you want to accomplish.

As well, the type of incense that you use can be entirely your personal preference. As mentioned in chapter two, certain types of incense can be used for various magical desires, but for example, if you associate strawberry incense with love and romance, then by all means use strawberry incense when doing a love spell. If you cannot make up your mind, sandalwood incense is an excellent all-purpose incense that will be effective with any kind of Bible magic spell.

As always, before you start your magic, place yourself in a quiet location so you won't be disturbed for about a half an hour. Relax and light your incense, envision the smoke rising as a caressing hand. Allow the incense to encircle your body and infuse your spirit with its wisdom and knowledge. Meditate on what you want your spell to accomplish and visualize how you will feel when your spell does its work. When you feel energized and ready, read your verse out loud three times. You can perform this spell for three days, wait three weeks, and try again if the spell does not take.

INCENSE SPELL TO TURN SADNESS INTO JOY

Suggested incense: frankincense

The works of the Lord are great, Studied by all who have pleasure in them, His work is honorable and glorious, And His righteousness endures forever, He has made His wonderful works to be remembered; The LORD is gracious and full of compassion

Psalms 111:2-4

INCENSE SPELL FOR PROTECTION IN YOUR HOME

Suggested incense: blue berry

For I am persuaded that neither death nor life, nor angels nor

principalities nor powers, nor things present nor things to come, nor

height nor depth, nor any other created thing, shall be able to

separate us from the love of God which is in Christ Jesus our Lord.

Romans 8:38-39

Forbidden Magic Spells From The Bible

INCENSE SPELL FOR PROTECTION WHEN YOU TRAVEL

Suggested incense: myrrh

For ye shall not go out in haste, neither shall ye go by flight: for Jehovah will go before you; and the God of Israel will be your rearward.

Isaiah 52:12

INCENSE SPELL TO PROTECT A LOVED ONE

Suggested incense: coconut

Yet even now, saith Jehovah, turn ye unto me with all your heart, and with fasting, and with weeping, and with mourning: and rend your heart, and not your garments, and turn unto Jehovah your God; for he is gracious and merciful, slow to anger, and abundant in lovingkindness, and repenteth him of the evil.

Joel 2:12-13

INCENSE SPELL TO CLEANSE THE SPIRIT

Suggested incense: lotus

He alone spreads out the heavens, And treads on the waves of the sea; He made the Bear, Orion, and the Pleiades, And the chambers of the south; He does great things past finding out, Yes, wonders without number.

Job 9:8-10

INCENSE SPELL TO IMPART KINDNESS IN A COLD HEART

Suggested incense: cedar

And he answered and said unto them, He that hath two coats, let him impart to him that hath none; and he that hath food, let him do likewise.

Luke 3:11

Forbidden Magic Spells From The Bible

INCENSE SPELL TO STOP THIEVES

Suggested incense: bayberry

Rob not the poor, because he is poor; Neither oppress the afflicted in the gate: For Jehovah will plead their cause, And despoil of life those that despoil them.

Proverbs 22:22

INCENSE SPELL TO KNOW THE TRUTH

Suggested incense: honeysuckle

And if thou sell aught unto thy neighbor, or buy of thy neighbor's hand, ye shall not wrong one another.

Leviticus 25:14

INCENSE SPELL FOR DEPRESSION AND LONELINESS

Suggested incense: valerian

Be sober, be watchful: your adversary the devil, as a roaring lion, walketh about, seeking whom he may devour, whom withstand stedfast in your faith, knowing that the same sufferings are accomplished in your brethren who are in the world.

1st Peter 5:8-9

INCENSE SPELL FOR FERTILITY

Suggested incense: musk

And he brought him forth abroad, and said, Look now toward heaven, and number the stars, if thou be able to number them: and he said unto him, So shall thy seed be.

Genesis 15:5

INCENSE SPELL TO CALM A TROUBLED YOUTH

Suggested incense: passionflower

These things command and teach. Let no man despise thy youth; but be thou an ensample to them that believe, in word, in manner of life, in love, in faith, in purity. Till I come, give heed to reading, to exhortation, to teaching.

1st Timothy 4:11-13

INCENSE SPELL TO INCREASE PSYCHIC POWERS

Suggested incense: cinnamon

For if the word spoken through angels proved stedfast, and every transgression and disobedience received a just recompense of reward; how shall we escape, if we neglect so great a salvation? which having at the first been spoken through the Lord, was confirmed unto us by them that heard; God also bearing witness with them, both by signs and wonders, and by manifold powers, and by gifts of the Holy Spirit, according to his own will.

Hebrews 2:2-4

INCENSE SPELL TO OPEN THE EYES OF THOSE WHO WILL NOT SEE

Suggested incense: peppermint

And it shall come to pass, if they will not believe even these two signs, neither hearken unto thy voice, that thou shalt take of the water of the river, and pour it upon the dry land: and the water which thou takest out of the river shall become blood up.

Exodus 4:9

INCENSE SPELL TO OBTAIN FAVORS FROM IMPORTANT PEOPLE

Suggested incense: patchouli

I communed with mine own hear, saying, Lo, I have gotten me great wisdom above all that were before me in Jerusalem; yea, my heart hath had great experience of wisdom and knowledge.

Ecclesiastes 1:16

INCENSE SPELL TO FIND INNER STRENGTH

Suggested incense: rosemary

Fear ye not me? saith Jehovah: will ye not tremble at my presence, who have placed the sand for the bound of the sea, by a perpetual decree, that it cannot pass it? and though the waves thereof toss themselves, yet can they not prevail; though they roar.

Jeremiah 5:22

INCENSE SPELL TO BE FREE OF UNCLEAN THOUGHTS AND DEEDS

Suggested incense: lavender

Depart ye, they cried unto them, Unclean! depart, depart, touch not! When they fled away and wandered, men said among the nations, They shall no more sojourn `here'.

Lamentations 4:15

INCENSE SPELL TO FIND TRUE AND LASTING LOVE

Suggested incense: jasmine

Many waters cannot quench love, Neither can floods drown it: If a man would give all the substance of his house for love, He would utterly be scorned.- Songofsongs 8:7

Forbidden Magic Spells From The Bible

INCENSE SPELL TO APPRECIATE LIFE TO ITS FULLEST

Suggested incense: rose

There is nothing better for a man `than' that he should eat and drink, and make his soul enjoy good in his labor. This also I saw, that it is from the hand of God.

Ecclesiastes 2:24

INCENSE SPELL TO SEND HEALING ENERGIES TO SOMEONE

Suggested incense: clove

And my God shall supply every need of yours according to his riches in glory in Christ Jesus.

Philippians 4:19

INCENSE SPELL TO HEAL ANY SICKNESS

Suggested incense: carnation

Ask, and it shall be given you; seek, and ye shall find; knock, and it shall be

opened unto you: for every one that asketh receiveth; and he that seeketh findeth; and to him that knocketh it shall be opened.

Matthew 7:7-8

INCENSE SPELL TO OVERCOME LIES AND SLANDER

Suggested incense: bay laurel

O Jehovah, thou hast persuaded me, and I was persuaded; thou art stronger than I, and hast prevailed: I am become a laughing-stock all the day, every one mocketh me.

Jeremiah 20:7

Forbidden Magic Spells From The Bible

INCENSE SPELL TO REMOVE ANY CURSE

Suggested incense: pine

And I will bring the blind by a way that they know not; in paths that they know not will I lead them; I will make darkness light before them, and crooked places straight. These things will I do, and I will not forsake them.

Isaiah 42:16

INCENSE SPELL TO PROTECT YOUR HOME FROM FIRE

Suggested incense: hazel

The Lord watches over you—the Lord is your shade at your right hand; the sun will not harm you by day, nor the moon by night. The Lord will keep you from all harm—he will watch over your life; the Lord will watch over your coming and going both now and forevermore.

Psalm 121:5-8

INCENSE SPELL FOR PROTECTION IN TIME OF WAR

Suggested incense: angelica

But now, this is what the Lord says — he who created you, O Jacob, he who formed you, O Israel: "Fear not, for I have redeemed you; I have summoned you by name; you are mine. When you pass through the waters, I will be with you; and when you pass through the rivers, they will not sweep over you. When you walk through the fire, you will not be burned; the flames will not set you ablaze.

Isaiah 43:1-2

Forbidden Magic Spells From The Bible

INCENSE SPELL TO BANISH EVIL SPIRITS

Suggested incense: violet

Put on the whole armor of God, that ye may be able to stand against the wiles of the devil.

Ephesians 6:11

INCENSE SPELL FOR SUCCESS IN MAKING MONEY

Suggested incense: cinnamon

Bring ye all the tithes into the storehouse, that there may be meat in mine house, and prove me now herewith, saith the Lord of hosts, if I will not open you the windows of heaven, and pour you out a blessing, that there shall not be room enough to receive it.

Malachi 3:10

INCENSE SPELL TO ATTRACT WEALTH

Suggested incense: ginger

Ask me, and I will give you the nations as your inheritance and the ends of the earth as your own possession.

Psalms 2:8

INCENSE SPELL FOR LUCK WITH THE LOTTERY

Suggested incense: chamomile

Honor the Lord with your possessions and with the first fruits of all your increase; so your barns will be filled with plenty, and your vats will overflow with new wine.

Proverbs 3:9-10

Forbidden Magic Spells From The Bible

INCENSE SPELL SO THAT DEBTS WILL BE REPAYED

Suggested incense: almond

Do not rob the poor because he is poor, nor oppress the afflicted at the gate; for the Lord will plead their cause, and plunder the soul of those who plunder them.

Proverbs 22:22-23

INCENSE SPELL TO GET A RAISE

Suggested incense: peony

Servants, in all things do the orders of your natural masters; not only when their eyes are on you, as pleasers of men, but with all your heart, fearing the Lord: Whatever you do, do it readily, as to the Lord and not to men.

Colossians 3:22-23

INCENSE SPELL TO FIND LOST MONEY

Suggested incense: marigold

Go, and cry in the ears of Jerusalem, saying, Thus saith Jehovah, I remember for thee the kindness of thy youth, the love of thine espousals; how thou wentest after me in the wilderness, in a land that was not sown.

Jeremiah 2:2

INCENSE SPELL TO NEVER HAVE MONEY WORRIES AGAIN

Suggested incense: patchouli

Give no occasions of stumbling, either to Jews, or to Greeks, or to the church of God: even as I also please all men in all things, not seeking mine own profit, but the `profit' of the many, that they may be saved.

1st Corinthians 10:32-33

Forbidden Magic Spells From The Bible

INCENSE SPELL TO RECEIVE INSTRUCTIONS IN DREAMS

Suggested incense: lavender

Surely then shalt thou lift up thy face without spot; Yea, thou shalt be stedfast, and shalt not fear: For thou shalt forget thy misery; Thou shalt remember it as waters that are passed away, And `thy' life shall be clearer than the noonday; Though there be darkness, it shall be as the morning.

Job 11:15-17

INCENSE SPELL TO FIND FORGIVENESS

Suggested incense: bayberry

And ye shall eat in plenty and be satisfied, and shall praise the name of Jehovah your God, that hath dealt wondrously with you; and my people shall never be put to shame.

Joel 2:26

INCENSE SPELL FOR A DESIRED RESULT

Suggested incense: ginger

For to this end we labor and strive, because we have our hope set on the living God, who is the Savior of all men, specially of them that believe. These things command and teach.

1st Timothy 4:10-11

INCENSE SPELL FOR GOOD LUCK AND HAPPINESS

Suggested incense: honeysuckle

I will give thanks unto thee; for I am fearfully and wonderfully made: Wonderful are thy works; And that my soul knoweth right well.

Psalms 139:14

Forbidden Magic Spells From The Bible

INCENSE SPELL TO BANISH ALL THAT WOULD DO HARM TO YOU OR ANY LOVED ONE

Suggested incense: rose

And be it still my consolation, Yea, let me exult in pain that spareth not, That I have not denied the words of the Holy One. What is my strength, that I should wait? And what is mine end, that I should be patient?

Job 6:10-11

INCENSE SPELL FOR NEW LOVE AND ROMANCE

Suggested incense: jasmine

I may be able to speak the languages of human beings and even of angels, but if I have no love, my speech is no more than a noisy gong or a clanging bell. I may have the gift of inspired preaching; I may have all knowledge and understand all secrets; I may have the faith needed to move mountains-but if I have no love, I am nothing. I may give away everything I have, and even give up my body to be burned-but if I have no love, this does me no good.

1 Corinthians, 13:1-13

INCENSE SPELL FOR AN EASY END TO A ROMANCE

Suggested incense: violet

And now, `though' thou wouldest needs be gone, because thou sore longedst after thy father's house, `yet' wherefore hast thou stolen my gods?

Genesis 31:30

INCENSE SPELL TO MEND A BROKEN HEART

Suggested incense: passionflower

He healeth the broken in heart, and bindeth up their wounds. He telleth the number of the stars; He calleth them all by their names. - Psalm 147:3-4

INCENSE SPELL TO RECEIVE INTUITIVE GUIDANCE WHEN MAKING AN IMPORTANT DECISION

Suggested incense: vanilla

For I know the plans I have for you, says the Lord. They are plans for good and not for evil, to give you a future and a hope.

Jeremiah 29:11

INCENSE SPELL TO TURN BAD LUCK INTO GOOD

Suggested incense: cinquefoil

And said, naked came I out of my mother's womb, and naked shall I return thither: the Lord gave, and the Lord hath taken away; blessed be the name of the Lord

Job 1:21

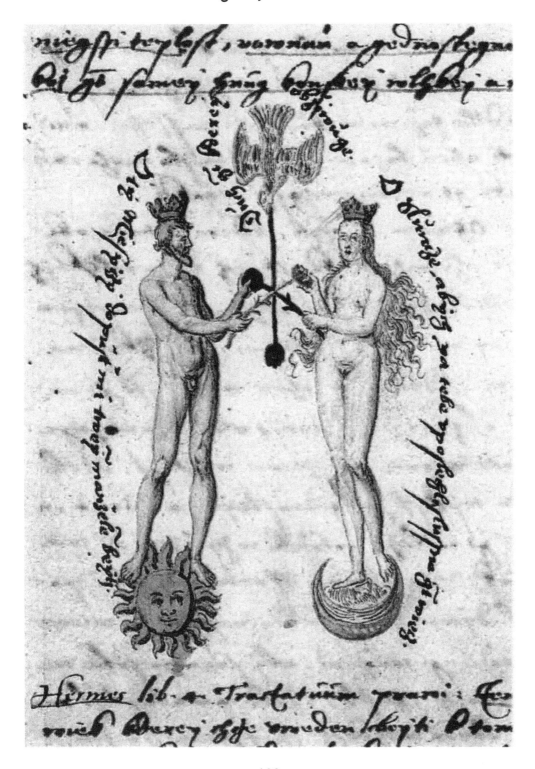

Forbidden Magic Spells From The Bible

VIII. A Family Tradition of Magic

FORBIDDEN BIBLE spells were zealously guarded by the Church Hierarchy for hundreds of years, yet despite the secrecy, they managed to leak out to the general population. After this point, there was no longer a hierarchy system, so it depended on the older generation to teach the next generation. Bible-based magic is now practiced as a family tradition and usually is handed down orally from person to person. It often hides behind more accepted belief systems associated with Christian tenets.

In compiling this book, I found that the spells used over the years have remained consistent despite the many different locations and families practicing this special form of magic. Because some churches teach their parishioners to react violently to anything they perceive as "magic," Bible spell practitioners have learned by unfortunate experience to remain low-key, despite the good that they do for their community.

In days when doctors and hospitals were few and far between, the "ol' granny lady" who could stop bleeding, or heal a baby's high fever using nothing more than a candle and a Bible verse was considered a God send by her neighbors. Nevertheless, when I asked many practitioners of Bible spell magic if they would share their knowledge for this book, many were hesitant because they did not want their special abilities to be known by anyone outside of the community. Some, though, were happy to share some of their own personal Bible spells that they had developed themselves.

TRADITIONAL BIBLE SPELLS

All practitioners of Bible-based magic follow the traditional spells that were handed down orally by their mothers and fathers. As well, everyone that I interviewed for this book confessed to coming up on their own, various personal Bible spells that were unique to them and them alone. In this final chapter, I decided to include some of these personal spells to show how any type of magic and ritual will develop, grow and change from generation to generation. While these personal spells were thought up by individuals to be used solely by themselves, when asked, no one thought that there should be any reason why anyone else could not also use these spells.

Because magic in all of its diverse forms are actually highly personal and dependent upon the creative energies brought forth by the practitioner, Bible-based magic is an excellent method for those who feel ready to attempt some spell creations of their own. You are part of creation, use that part of you that you share with the Creator to try a little special magic in your own life.

Say for instance that you want a unique Bible spell to cure a burn. Try closing your eyes, open your Bible and drop your finger onto the page. The verse your finger is on will be your special "burn cure" verse. Or you could pick a verse that just feels right to you.

Life is a mystery, the ultimate mystery. Knowledge is hidden and available only to those who are ready to listen. What we think we know today about religion, spirituality and the Universe is simply the surface of a greater meaning that is as deep and mysterious as the furthest reaches of our own subconscious.

Cure for the Colic

Take one fresh chicken egg and turn the small end three times in the navel of the sick baby. Say this Bible verse out loud over the baby: *Behold, if a river overflow, he trembleth not; He is confident, though a Jordan swell even to his mouth.* **Job 40:23**

Then bury the egg on the North end of the house. The mother of the baby should then burn a white onion in hog lard and remove the burnt pieces. Mash this up to make a salve and rub this on the baby's stomach morning and night for nine days.

Grandma Jenny, Southern Illinois

Forbidden Magic Spells From The Bible

STOP PAIN

Find a smooth creek stone big enough to fit into the palm of your hand. Hold the stone on the forehead of the one who is in pain and say the following chant: *Hair and hide, Flesh and blood, Nerve and bone, No more pain than this stone.*

Next say the following Bible verse: *and they lifted up their voices, saying, Jesus, Master, have mercy on us.* **Luke 17:13**

Robert Cooke, Paducah, Kentucky

TO LIFT A CURSE

If someone complains of being cursed, lay your hands on their shoulders and silently say the following: *Lord Jesus, thy wounds so red will guard me against death. Lord Jesus, thy suffering so profound will guard me against pain. Lord Jesus, thy tears so cleansing will guard me against evil.*

Maddie Gunselman, Youngstown, Ohio

TO RELEASE SOMEONE WHO IS SPELL-BOUND

This can be done for someone who is in your presence or at a distance. If the person is far-away, make sure no creek or river is between you. Say this out loud: *You horseman and footman, whom I here conjured at this time, you may pass on in the name of Jesus Christ, through the word of God and the will of Christ; ride ye on now and pass.*

Next, read this Bible verse to yourself: *Unto the upright there ariseth light in the darkness: He is' gracious, and merciful, and righteous.* **Psalms 112:4**

Joseph Jerger, Cross Roads, Pennsylvania

Forbidden Magic Spells From The Bible

TO BE BLESSED AT ALL TIMES

To be assured of Gods blessing everyday, say this silently to yourself in the morning upon arising from bed: *I conjure thee, sword, sabre or knife, that mightest injure or harm me, by the priest of all prayers, who had gone into the temple at Jerusalem, and said: An edged sword shall pierce your soul that you may not injure me, who am a child of God.*

TO ASSURE GOD'S BLESSING TO A LOVED ONE

If there is someone you love and want them to receive God's blessing and protection, without telling them what you are doing, say their name out loud when the sun rises in the morning and then say silently: *Like unto the cup and the wine, and the holy supper, which our dear Lord Jesus Christ gave unto his dear disciples on Maunday Thursday, may the Lord Jesus guard [name] in daytime, and at night, that no dog may bite [name], no wild beast tear [name] to pieces, no tree fall on [name], no water rise against [name], no fire-arms injure [name], no weapons, no steel, no iron, cut [name], no fire burn [name], no false sentence fall upon [name], no false tongue injure [name], no rogue enrage [name], and that no fiends, no witchcraft and enchantment can harm [name]. Amen.*

Katherine Nedpepper, Southern Michigan

TO SPELL-BIND ANYTHING

Say the Lord's Prayer three times. Then say: *Christ's cross and Christ's crown, Christ Jesus' colored blood, be thou every hour good. God, the Father, is before me; God, the Son, is beside me; God, the Holy Ghost, is behind me. Whoever now is stronger than these three persons may come, by day or night, to attack me.*

Leonard Arvin, Raglesville, Indiana

Forbidden Magic Spells From The Bible

A CURE FOR WOUNDS

Take the bones of a calf, and burn them until they turn to powder, and then strew it into the wound. Next, recite this Bible verse: *Receive him therefore in the Lord with all joy; and hold such in honor: because for the work of Christ he came nigh unto death, hazarding his life to supply that which was lacking in your service toward me.* **Philippians 2:29-30**

The powder prevents the flesh from putrefying, and is therefore of great importance in healing the wound.

Another cure is for cuts and scratches on a child. Place both of your hands on the head of a hurt child and say: *Mother Mary stop thy crying, Mother Mary stop thy pain. With your son's blood speak truth from these lips.*

Stephanie Schnell, Knob Fork, West Virginia

A REMEDY FOR BURNS

To relieve the pain and heal a burn, say this Bible verse to yourself: *Now the God of hope fill you with all joy and peace in believing, that ye may abound in hope, in the power of the Holy Spirit.* **Romans 15:13**

Next, say this out loud: *Clear out, brand, but never in; be thou cold or hot, thou must cease to burn. May God guard thy blood and thy flesh, thy marrow and thy bones, and every artery, great or small. They all shall be guarded and protected in the name of God against inflammation and mortification, in the name of God the Father, the Son, and the Holy Ghost. Amen.*

This can be done in the presence of those that are injured, or to heal someone from a distance.

Eugene Schoephorster, Bloomfield, Missouri

A WAY TO FIND LOVE FOR THOSE WHO SEEK

Take a piece of red ribbon and wrap it three times around the wrist of those seeking love. With each wrap, say these words: *Oh Song of Songs find thee love. Oh Song of Songs bring thee love. Oh Song of Songs keep thee love.*

Wear the ribbon for three days and at the end of the third day, remove the ribbon and place it in a Bible to insure God's blessing.

Almeda Kieffner, Bethpage, Tennessee

KEEP POVERTY AT BAY

To keep poverty from taking everything away from you or a friend, take a length of black thread from an unused spool. Starting from the bottom, tie seven knots throughout the length of the thread and recite out loud with each knot: *For we are God's workmanship, created in Christ Jesus to do good works, which God prepared in advance for us to do.* **Ephesians 2:10**

Place the thread in a small bag and whoever needs it, carry it with him at all times to keep poverty away.

Marylyn Davis, Marshal, Illinois

FOR A DIFFICULT PREGNANCY

If a woman is worried that the baby she is carrying will be premature or breach, take a bowl of fresh rainwater and dip your finger in it. With your wet finger, make the sign of the cross on the stomach of the pregnant woman and say out loud: *May it please thee O, Eel Chad, to grant unto this woman [name] daughter of [name], that she may not at this time, or at any other time, have a premature confinement; much more grant unto her a truly fortunate delivery, and keep her and the fruit of the body in good health.*

If a woman is having trouble conceiving, say this: *Lord and Lady. Mother and Father. Life Divine. Gift [name] with a healthy child.*

William Kleinhelter, Sugar Grove, Kentucky

116

Forbidden Magic Spells From The Bible

TO HAVE GOOD FORTUNE

This is for anyone who has been unlucky despite their best efforts. Say this Bible verse three times before the sun rises: *And they that are wise shall shine as the brightness of the firmament; and they that turn many to righteousness as the stars for ever and ever.* **Daniel 12:3**

Sarah Knies, Altay, New York

TO CURE SICKNESS IN A PET OR FARM ANIMAL

Run your hand along the back of a sick animal while saying: *To Desh break no Flesh, but to Desh!*

The hand must be put upon the bare skin in all cases of using sympathetic words.

Marcus Dunkel, Leland, Wisconsin

TO OVERCOME WICKED PEOPLE

To stop anyone who means to do you or your loved ones harm, say the following Bible verse: *One of themselves, a prophet of their own, said, Cretans are always liars, evil beasts, idle gluttons.* **Titus 1:12**

Sophia Beckman, Wick, Ohio

PROTECT YOUR HOME AND BELONGINGS

Write the following sacred names on a clean piece of white paper: Write the following on a piece of white paper: SATOR, AREPO, TENET, OPERA, ROTAS. Seal them in a small bag that can be tied or sewn shut. Place the bag near your front door.

Daniel Jochem, Locke, Indiana

Forbidden Magic Spells From The Bible

WAYS OF THE WORLD

Cats and dogs will not go into a room where there are spirits and ghosts present; Death comes in threes to a family or community; If you tell a bad dream before breakfast it will come true; If you whistle before breakfast, you will cry before dusk; If you dream of death it's a sign of a birth, if you dream of birth, it's a sign of death.

Rosalie Tyler, Elwood, Indiana

TO LIVE HAPPY AND BE PROSPEROUS

Say this verse once a day, every day: *Thou wilt shew me the path of life; in thy presence is fullness of joy; at thy right hand there are pleasures for evermore.* **Psalms 16:11**

Lena Bell, Mount Crest, Tennessee

THE MAGICAL WRITINGS OF THE GREAT MAGICIAN

HAVING LIVED many years free from worry and despair, it falls upon to reveal the great secrets and hidden knowledge that have been passed down to me by my forbearers. Since this knowledge has afforded me times of absolute joy and happiness, destiny compels that this happiness be shared with those deserving to learn these arcane secrets of the ancients.

Others have taken some of these great teachings and have tried to profit with books claiming to be by their own hand. But do not be taken in by these thieves of the night, their charms and incantations are tainted with the black foulness of greed and deception. The words in this fine book are indeed ancient and true of spirit, given from father to son for untold generations since the times when the angels first brought them from God's loving hand to his chosen people.

I hereby commit to the perusal of the reader a collection of great secrets, sufficient in number as may be deemed needful for any purposes. Knowing, from experience, how many an honest citizen hath been robbed of his entire estate through the machination of bad and malicious people, how many a man hath been tortured and tantalized at night, from early childhood, by wicked people of that ilk; so much so that they could hardly bear it any longer. If you are good and true of heart, the great secrets contained within this little book will release you of all troubles, whether they be troubles of this world, or the worlds of spirits both clean and unclean.

Whenever said remedy is to be applied, in case the house of him whom it is intended to assist is called aloud three times with devotion, and by adding both his Christian and all his other names, the usefulness thereof will be readily enough perceived. Thus it happens that this collection contains a number of curious performances of magic, every one of which is worth far more than the reader pays for this entire book.

For the purpose of rendering a great service to mankind, this book was issued, in order to bridle and check the doings of the spirits of wickedness. Whatever objections may be raised against this book by disbelief and jealousy, these pages will, despite all such objections, contain naught else but truth divine, since Christ himself hath commanded that all ye may perform, ye shall do in the name of God, the Son, and the Holy Spirit, so that the Devil may not possess any power over anything whatso-ever to do his will.

I, therefore, beseech every one, into whose hands this book may come, not to treat the same lightly or to destroy the same, because, by such action, he will defy the will of God. Do not use this book to gain power or take any property that belongs to someone else. Neither will you use this book to bring harm to others in any way. To do so will surely bring about the wraith of God with quick and unmerciful judgment and eternal punishment. So to him who properly esteems and values this book, and never abuses its teachings, will not only be granted the usefulness of its contents, but he will also attain everlasting joy and blessing.

Wherever the "2 N. N." occurs, both the baptismal name and all other names of him whom you intend to help, aid or assist, will have to be added, while the † † † signify the highest name of God, which should always be added in conclusion. Every sympathetic formula should be repeated three times.

A WONDERFUL PRAYER TO INSURE A HAPPY AND PROSPEROUS LIFE

Say this prayer every morning upon rising:

This grant God the Father, God the Son, and God the Holy Spirit. Now I will rise in the name of the Lord, and will wander in his path by his word and will beseech our Savior Christ that he may lend me, upon this very day, three of his angels, for this I pray; the first he may protect me, the other keep me without weapon or arms, the third may keep my body from all harm and keep my soul, my blood and flesh, and keep my courage ever fresh. Whoever is stronger as Jesus Christ, he may approach and assail my flesh and blood. In the name of God the Father, the Son and the Holy Ghost. I praise thee heavenly host. This may grant God the Father, God the Son, and God the Holy Spirit. † † †

BENEDICTION TO PROTECT FROM THE DANGERS OF ANY SORT OF WEAPON

Jesus, the true God and man, protect me, N. N., from all sorts of arms and weapons, be they of iron, steel, lead, or be they nails, knives or wood, whatever was made and grew since the birth of Christ, is now forged, or may yet be forged, at any future time, of whatever material. Jesus Christ, the true God and man, protect me, N. N., from murder and from cannon balls, from bullets and swords, from thunder and lightning, fire and water, chains and prison, from poison and sorcery, from mad dogs and from shedding of blood, and from sudden death. Save me, Lord God. Jesus, the true God and man, protect me, N. N., from all sorts of arms and weapons, and all those who desire to overpower me. Cause that all their might and strength to be lost, and be vain.

N. N., hold and aim your armament and sword or lancet toward the cross of Christ and his sacred five wounds, in all my troubles, and at all times; and command all shot and fire-arms that they may fail to give fire; and all swords, spears, lancets, and hellebards, and other pointed instruments, that their edges may become as soft as the blood of Christ, who suffered on the cross. Jesus, protect N. N., wherever I may be, against all enemies, be they visible or invisible, secret or open. The eternal Godhead may save and protect me through the bitter sufferings, death and resurrection of Jesus Christ, and through his holy rose-colored blood, which he shed upon the cross. Jesus begotten at Nazareth, born in Bethlehem, died in Jerusalem, crucified and tortured; these are truthful words, which are written in this letter, that I may not be captured by any murderer, or any other man, be killed, whipped, wounded, nor be laid in fetters; let move away from me, or yield my will. Fly and vanish until I shall recall them, all enemies and all arms, weapons and armament, may they be called by whatever name. None will injure me. Lead and iron projectiles, remain quiet in your armament, for the sake of the martyred Jesus Christ and his holy five wounds. In the name of the Father, the Son and the Holy Spirit. In case a person has a tumor growing, or warts of any kind upon his body, he or she shall go to church and, when he notices two persons speaking to each other, he shall touch the humor or wart, and recite three times: What I see is a great sin and shame, and what I touch may vanish soon.

Forbidden Magic Spells From The Bible

TO PROTECT ALL POSSESSIONS FROM THIEVES

Speak this every morning three times over all possessions:

Our dear mother in a garden came. Three angels comforted her there. The first is named St. Michael; the other, St. Gabriel; the third, St. Peter. Then spake Peter to our beloved Mary: I saw three thieves enter there. They intend to steal thy dear child and kill it. But the beloved mother Mary said: Peter, bind; St. Peter, bind; and Peter bound them with iron bands, with God's own hands, and with his holy five wounds, for this be with Gabriel, upon this day and night, and this entire year, and forever and all times, my possessions bound. Whoever attempts to steal therefrom, must stand still, like a stick, and see like a brick, and must stand quiet. He must go upward, that he cannot depart from hence until I permit him to proceed from thence. With my own tongue I must tell him this. This is my order and Gabriel's will, which now, by day and night, and all the year, for all times to come, will utter to every thief, for them to repent. For this may God his blessing lend. God the Father, God the Son, and God the Holy Spirit. Amen.

PRAYER TO BE SECURED FROM ALL ASSAILANTS

Now I will Walk over the threshold I met three men, not yet very old. The first was God the Father; the other was God the Son; the third was God the Holy Spirit. They protect my body and soul, blood and flesh, that in no well I fall, that water may not swell me at all, that a rabid dog may never bite me, that shot and stone may never smite me, that spear and knife may never cut me; that never a thief may steal the least from me. Then it shall become like our dear Savior's sweat. Whoever is stronger and mightier than these three men, he may come hither, assail me if he can, or forever keep his peace with me. † † †

TO SECURE AGAINST ATTACK WHILE TRAVELING

Speak three times: *Two wicked eyes have overshadowed me, but three other eyes are overshadowing me too, the one of God, the Father, the other of God the Son, the third of God the Holy Spirit, they watch my blood and flesh, my marrow and bone, and all other large and small limbs, they shall be protected in the name of God the Holy Spirit, God the Father, God the Son. † † †*

Forbidden Magic Spells From The Bible

TO PREVENT ANYONE FROM DOING EVIL AGAINST YOU

Welcome, in the name of God, ye brethren true and God, we all have drank of the Savior's blood. God the Father be with me; God the Son be with you; God the Holy Spirit be with us all. Let us meet in union and part from each other in peace. † † † Three times spoken.

HOW TO PREDICT THE FUTURE STATE OF THE WEATHER DURING THE YEAR

If New-Year's Day falls upon a Sunday, a quiet and gloomy winter may be expected, followed by a stormy spring, a dry summer, and a rich vintage. When New-Year's Day comes on a Monday, a varied winter, good spring, dry summer, cloudy weather, and an inferior vintage may be expected. When New-Year's comes on a Wednesday, a hard, rough winter, a blustery, dreary spring, an agreeable summer, and a blessed vintage may be hoped for. If the first of the year happens to come on Thursday, a temperate winter, agreeable spring, a dry summer, and a very good vintage will follow. If on a Friday the year begins, a changeable, irregular winter, a fine spring, a dry and comfortable summer, and a rich harvest will be the result. If New-Year's Day comes on Saturday, a rough winter, bleak winds, a wet and dreary spring, and destruction of fruit will be the consequence.

TO OBTAIN MONEY

Take the eggs of a swallow, boil them, return them to the nest, and if the old swallow brings a root to the nest, take it, put it into your purse, and carry it in your pocket, and be happy.

TO OPEN ALL LOCKS

Kill a green frog, expose it to the sun for three days, powder or pulverize it. A little of this powder put into a lock will open the same.

HOW TO DISCERN ALL SECRETS AND INVISIBLE THINGS

If you find a white adder under a hazelnut shrub, which had twelve other vipers as its twelve guardsmen with it, and the hazelnut bush, under which they lay, bears commonly medlers, you must eat the white adder with your other food, and you will be enabled to see and discern all secret and otherwise hidden things.

HOW TO STOP BLEEDING

Jesus born at Bethlehem, Jesus crucified at Jerusalem, as true as these words are, to truly understand N. N. (here call the name of him whom you desire to help) that thy blood will now be stopped, in the name of God the Father, the Son, and the Holy Spirit.

HOW TO CAUSE YOUR INTENDED WIFE TO LOVE YOU

Take feathers from a rooster's tail and press them three times into her hand.

Or: Take a turtle dove tongue into your mouth, talk to your friend agreeably, kiss her and she will love you so dearly that she will never love another.

WHEN YOU WISH THAT YOUR SWEETHEART SHALL NOT DENY YOU

Take the turtle dove tongue into your mouth again and kiss her, and she will accept your suit.

Or: Take salt, cheese and flour, mix it together, put it into her room, and she will rest not until she sees you.

Forbidden Magic Spells From The Bible

PRAYER TO HEAL MAN AND BEAST FROM ATTACKS BY EVIL SPIRITS

Thou unclean spirit, thou has attacked N. N.; let that witchcraft recede from him into thy marrow and into thy bone, let it be returned unto thee. I exorcise thee for the sake of the five wounds of Jesus, thou evil spirit, and conjure thee for the five wounds of Jesus of this flesh, marrow and bone; I exorcise thee for the sake of the five wounds of Jesus, at this very hour restore to health again N. N., in the name of God the Father, God the Son, and of God the Holy Spirit. Speak this three times over said victim during three sunrises.

PRAYER TO FOREVER BANISH WICKED PEOPLE

All ye evil spirits, I forbid you my bedstead, my couch; I forbid you, in the name of God, my house and home; I forbid you, in the name of the Holy Trinity, my blood and flesh, my body and soul; I forbid you all the nail holes in my house and home, till you have traveled over every hillock, waded through every water, have counted all the leaflets of the trees, and counted all the starlets in the sky, until that beloved day arrives when the mother of God will bring forth her second Son. † † †

This prayer, three times spoken in the house of the bewitched person, always adding, in the right place, both his baptismal and other names, has been found excellent in many cases.

TO HEAL INJURIES ON MAN, CATTLE OR HORSE

Cut down a burdock bush, and put it into your house, so that it may wither. Then take a thread from a reel which had never been washed, and speak:

Burdock bush, I bind thee that thou shalt heal the injury of this man (or beast, as the case may be), be it boils, sores, gout, swellings, or whatever it may be. Double the thread, and move around the bush, where the thickest part is, in the name of God the Father, and make a knot, then repeat the same in the name of God the Son, and make another knot, and repeat the same motion, while saying in the name of the Holy Spirit, and again make a knot, and say then: What I and thou cannot heal, that may heal the Holy Trinity.

After this, put the bush in a place where no air moves, and the injury will be healed from the root.

TO MAKE ONE'S SELF SHOT PROOF

Dig and stick mouse-ear herb on a Friday, during the half or full of the moon, tie in a white cloth and suspend it from the body. Probatum.

Or carry these words upon your body:

LIGHT, BETTER, CLOTENTAL,

SOBATH, ADONAY,

ALBOA, FLOBAT

TO SEE WHAT OTHERS CANNOT SEE

Take a cat's eye, lay it in salt water, let it remain there for three days, and then for six days into the rays of the sun, after this have it set in silver, and hang it around your neck.

AN AMBROSE-STONE

Steal the eggs of a raven, boil them hard, lay them again into the nest and the raven will fly across the sea and bring a stone from abroad and lay it over the eggs and they will become at once soft again. If such a stone is wrapped up into a bay leaf and is given to a prisoner, that prisoner will be liberated at once. Whoever touches a door with such a stone, to him that door will be opened, and he who puts that stone into his mouth will understand the song of every bird.

Forbidden Magic Spells From The Bible

WHEN A CHILD IS BEWITCHED

Stand with the child toward the morning sun, and speak:

Be welcome In God's name and sunshine, from whence didst brightly beam, aid me and my dear child and feign my songs serenely stream. To keep the Father sound my praise, help praise the Holy Ghost that he restore my child to health, I praise the heavenly host. † † †

TO ALLAY PAINS WHEREVER THEY BE

Today is a holy sacred day, that God will not cause you any pain to bear, which thou may have on any part of your body, be it man, horse, cattle, or anything living, all the same. I beseech thee. Oh, holy Trinity, help this N. N., that all his pains may cease, whatever they may be called and all that Cometh from evil things. Christ commandeth, Christ vanquisheth, Christ became a being in flesh for thy sake and to protect thee against all evil. Jesus Christ of Nazareth, the crucified Saviour, with Mary his beloved mother, help this N. N. from all evil whatever name it may bear. Amen, † † †

Jesus Nazarenus Rex Judaeorum.

TO MAKE A MIRROR IN WHICH EVERYTHING MAY BE DISCERNED

Procure a looking glass, such as are commonly sold. Inscribe the characters noted below upon it. Inter it on the crossing of two pathways, during an uneven hour. On the third day thereafter, return to the place at same hour, and take it out: but you must not be the first person to look into the glass. It is best to let a dog or a cat take the first look into the mirror:

S. Solam S. Tattler S. Echogardner Gematar.

TO ASCERTAIN WHETHER OR NOT A SICK PERSON WILL DIE

Take a piece of bread, place it before the sick one's brow, then throw it before a dog. If he eats it, the patient recovers; if he rejects it, the sick one dies.

TO DRIVE AWAY AND VANQUISH ALL FOES

Whoever carries the hemlock herb, with the heart of a mole, on his person, vanquishes all his enemies, so that they will not be able to trouble him.' Such a man will obtain much. When this herb is laid under the head of a sick person, the sick one, when he sings, will get well; if he cries, he will die.

WHILE TRAVELING

Say every morning:

Grant me, oh Lord, a good and pleasant hour, that all sick people may recover, and all distressed in body or mind, repose or grace may find, and guardian angel may over them hover; and all those captive and in bondage fettered; may have their conditions and troubles bettered; to all good travelers on horse or foot, we wish a safe journey joyful and good, and good women in labor and toil a safe delivery and joy. † † †

A WAND TO DISCOVER TREASURE

Proceed in the forenoon before twelve o'clock to a hazelnut shrub, which grew within one year and has two twigs, then place yourself toward the rising sun and take the twigs in both hands and speak:

I conjure thee, one summer long, hazel rods by the power of God, by the obedience of Jesus Christ of Nazareth, God and Mary's own son, who died on the cross, and by the power of God, by the truth of God arose from the dead; God the Father, Son and Holy Ghost, who art the very truth thyself, that thou showest me where silver and gold is hidden.

The twigs will now move whenever in the presence of treasure.

Forbidden Magic Spells From The Bible

HOW TO TELL A PERSON'S FORTUNE WITH CARDS

The Romany have for centuries used this method of telling fortunes with playing cards to make money off of the outsiders. Only those within the tribes know the true secrets of how to use the cards to discern the future. As many of those events about to happen may be easily gathered from the cards, I have here affixed the definition which each card in the pack bears separately; by combining them the reader must judge for himself, observing the following directions in laying them out.

It is worked with a piquet set of ordinary playing cards, which, as most people will know, consists of the usual picture-pieces and the ace, 10, 9, 8 and 7 of each suit, excluding the lower numbers.

DIAMONDS

The Ace. -Letters, or news at hand otherwise.

King. -Friendship; if followed by the Queen, marriage; if reversed, impediments, difficulties and the vexations thereto belonging.

Queen. -A woman from the country, who is fair but evil-speaking; reversed, more directly inimical to the Querent in word and also in deed.

Knave. -A postman, valet, postillion, soldier, or messenger bearing news. The news are good if the card is right side up and bad if it appears reversed. Ten. - Great joy, change of place, a party from the country.

Nine. -Delay and postponement, but not resulting in failure.

Eight. -A man of business or young merchant, who is commercially related to the Querent.

Seven. -Good news, above all if accompanied by the Ace.

HEARTS

The Ace. -Joy, contentment, and if it is accompanied by several picture-cards, marriages, feasts, etc;, in pleasant company.

King. -A rich man, banker, or financier, well disposed, and may promote the interests of the Querent. If reversed, the person is miserly and to deal with him will prove difficult.

Queen. -An honest, frank and obliging woman; if reversed, there will be some obstacle to a projected marriage.

Knave. -A soldier or young man, who is anxious to promote the Querent's welfare, will play some part in his life and will be allied with him after one or another manner.

Ten. -A surprise, but often one of a kind which will be advantageous as well as agreeable to the consulting party.

Nine. -Concord.

Eight. -Domestic and private happiness, attended by success in undertakings; exceedingly felicitous for the destinies of the middle path, the amenities of the quiet life.

Seven. -Marriage, if the Querent is a lady and the issue will be daughters only; if a man, it is destined that he will make a rich and happy marriage.

SPADES

The Ace. -In company with the ten and nine, this card signifies death, grief, more especially from bereavement, but also sorrow from many sources; it includes further the idea of treason and possibly of loss by theft or robbery.

King. -A magistrate or lawyer, whose intervention may prove disagreeable; the card reversed signifies loss in a lawsuit or general derangement of affairs.

Queen. -A disappointed woman – possibly a widow in dejection; if reversed, one who is anxious to remarry, unknown to or in spite of her family.

Knave. -Some kind of disgrace which will be inimical to the peace of mind and perhaps even the liberty of the Querent; reversed, serious complications for the person concerned; also betrayal in love, if the Querent is a woman.

Ten. -Imprisonment for a man, if followed by the Ace and King of the same suit; for a woman, disease, illness.

Nine. -Protraction and difficulties in business; followed by the Nine of Diamonds and the Ace of Clubs, delay in the receipt of expected money.

Eight. -Arrival of a person who will carry bad news if followed by the Seven of Diamonds and near to a picture card- whether King, Queen or Knave- tears, discord, destitution or loss of employment.

Seven. -Quarrels, inquietude; if ameliorated by the vicinity of some Hearts, it promises safety, independence and moral consolation.

Forbidden Magic Spells From The Bible

CLUBS

The Ace. -Advantages, commercial and industrial benefits of every kind, easy collection of dues, unmixed prosperity – but these more especially when followed by the Seven of Diamonds and the Seven of Clubs.

King. -An influential, powerful person, who is equitable and benevolent towards the Querent, to whom he will render signal services; but reversed this personage will experience some difficulty in his proceedings and may be even in danger of failure.

Queen. -A dark woman, rivalry, competitive spirit; in the neighborhood of a card which stands for a man, she will have preference for the man in question; on the contrary, in proximity to a feminine card, she will be in sympathy with the Querent; reversed, she is very covetous, jealous and disposed to infidelity.

Knave. -One who is in love, a proper young man, who pays court to a young lady; placed next to a feminine card, his chances of success are very good; side by side with a man, there is reason to hope that the latter will come actively to his assistance and will contribute to his success, unless the said man should be signified by the Knave of Hearts, which presages a dangerous rivalry; reversed, there is reason to fear opposition to marriage on the part of the person's parents.

Ten. -Prosperity and good fortune of every kind; at the same time, if followed by the Nine of Diamonds a delay is foreshadowed in the return of money; contrary to all, if this card is side by side with the Nine of Spades – which everywhere signifies disappointment complete failure is promised; so also if the question at stake is a lawsuit, loss is probable.

Nine. -Success in love; for a bachelor or spinster, approaching marriage; for a widow, her second nuptials.

Eight. -A favorable conclusion which may be anticipated by the Querent in financial and business matters.

Seven. -Anxieties occasioned by love -- intrigues; followed by the Seven of Diamonds and the Nine of Spades, abundance of good things and rich family inheritances.

SOME EXAMPLES ON HOW THE CARDS CAN BE USED

FOR MARRIAGE AND AFFAIRS OF THE HEART

Shuffle the cards of a piquet set and cut three times. If an actual marriage is in question, remove two cards, representing the lover and the lady whose fortunes are at issue. Place these cards, face upwards, on the table before you. As usual, fair people are represented by Hearts and Diamonds but those of dark complexion by Clubs and Spades. The attribution, between these lines, seems to be usually at predilection or discretion, but Diamonds are sometimes taken to signify very fair people and blondes, while Spades are for actual brunettes and very dusky complexions.

Lay out the rest of the cards three by three; in every triplicity which produces two of the same suit, select the higher card of that suit and place it by the side of the other card which stands for the Querent. Throw out the rest for the moment, but they will be required later. When any triplicity produces entirely different suits, put aside all three in the rejected pile. When the entire cards of the set have thus been dealt with in succession, take up the rejected lot, and after shuffling and cutting as before, proceed in the same manner until you have drawn fifteen cards and placed them by the side of the Querent.

If the Querent is a dark man, he will not have his wish regarding the marriage contemplated unless a tierce to the King in Clubs be among the fifteen cards. It may of course happen that the King has been drawn to represent him. If, however; he be a Spade, then alternatively there must be a tierce in Spades. The same rule obtains if the Querent is a dark young lady, but in addition to a tierce in the suit there must be the Ace of the suit also.

If the Querent is a fair man or woman, then a tierce in the one case and a tierce and the Ace in the other must be found in Hearts or Diamonds according to the grade of their fairness. If the question concerns a marriage to take place in the country, it has been held by the expositors of the system that a tierce to the King in Diamonds is indispensable. This seems to involve the system in respect of fair people, but it is only a confusion of expression.

If Diamonds correspond to the Querent, that tierce must obviously be present, or there will be no marriage; but if present the inference is that the Querent will get his wish in respect of locality as well as of the fact of marriage. On the other hand, if the Querent is referable to any other of the three remaining suits, then ex hypothesi to attain his presumed wish for a country wedding, he must have the tierce in Diamonds as well as in his own suit.

It is not very probable that the alternative between town and country will arise as a subsidiary question, and if it does, it might be better to determine it separately by the help of some other system. It serves no purpose to ignore the shades of complexion in fair people and represent them indifferently by Diamonds, as this would be forcing the oracles and would make the reading void.

Finally, if the marriage question concerns a widower or widow, it is equally essential that the cards drawn should furnish a tierce to the King in Spades and the Ace of Hearts- which again is very hard upon all persons who are not represented by Spades. The inference is that second marriages are rare.

FOR QUESTIONS ON INHERITANCES

Shuffle and cut as before, and place on the table a card which is held to typify the Querent. The presence of the Ace of Spades, manifesting right side up, indicates profit in consequence of a death that is to say, an inheritance or legacy. If the Ace is accompanied by the Seven, Eight, Nine and Ten of Clubs, there will be a large increment of money. The combination may be difficult to secure, but very large inheritances are rarer than second marriages.

Forbidden Magic Spells From The Bible

FOR LAWSUITS AND SIMILAR MATTERS

No judgment can be given on the chances of a lawsuit, actual or pending, nor generally on things of this nature, unless the King of Spades comes out in the dealing. If that card is held usually to represent the Querent, then it only follows automatically that a judgment is possible, and it is so much the easier for him in such case.

The shuffling, cutting and dealing proceed as before, and if the Ace in question serves to complete the quint major in Spades – that is, the Ace, King, Queen, Knave and Ten – it is to be feared that the suit will prove good for nothing, either by going against the Querent or bringing him no profit in the opposite case. But if the Ace is accompanied by the four Tens, the chances are excellent.

They are said also to be more than good in another event of the dealing which I forbear from dwelling on, as it is practically, if not otherwise, impossible for the fifteen cards – which the dealing proposes to extract – to be all of the red suits. It is well known that compilers of works on cartomancy sometimes forget the limits prescribed by their systems and get consequently into ridiculous plights.

FOR A THEFT

For the discovery of a thief, the presence of the four Knaves is indispensable to any reading, and, as it happens, it is not utterly difficult – though it is none too easy – that the chances of the cards should produce them.

The procedure is throughout as before. If the King and the Eight of Spades turn up among the fifteen cards, this means that the thief is already in prison; if the Ace of Spades is among them, the prisoner will be in danger of death; the presence of the Ace of Clubs, the King of Clubs and the Queen of Hearts will afford some hope that the person who stole will himself make restitution; lastly, the predominance of Diamonds offers ground for believing that the thief has been arrested, but on another charge than that which would be preferred by the Querent on his own part.

Forbidden Magic Spells From The Bible

FOR A PERSON IN PRISON

The question at issue is whether the captive has any chance of speedy liberation. The procedure is throughout as before, except that the card selected is held to represent the person in durance instead of the Querent. The fifteen cards having been produced as the result of the working, they should be examined in the usual way. The presence of the Queen of Hearts, Knave of Clubs, Nine of Clubs and the four Aces will give ground for hope that liberation will be easy and at hand.

In proportion as these cards are absent, there will be delay in the desired event, and if none are found, it is likely to be rather remote. On the other hand, the appearance of the Eight and Nine of Spades, the King of Spades, and the Knave and Nine of Diamonds, will signify that liberty shall be scarcely obtained, except after many obstacles and much consequent postponement.

FOR TRAVELERS

It is assumed that the Querent is not himself on a journey but is consulting the oracles for one in whose fortunes he is for some reason interested, by ties of friendship or otherwise. Proceed as before, selecting a card to represent the absent person. When the dealing is finished, the resulting cards should be consulted to ascertain whether they include the Ace of Hearts, the Ace of Diamonds and the Ten of Diamonds, the presence of which will foreshadow probable news. Probability will be raised into certainty by the appearance of the Seven of Diamonds. If, however, the Ten of Spades is found in proximity to the card representing the person who is away on his travels, there will be reason to fear that he is ill; so also the Ace of Spades reversed will mean that he is in other danger than sickness. If he is to succeed in the enterprise that has called him abroad, he will be escorted by the Nine of Hearts, the Ace and the King of Clubs. Finally, if the Eight of Diamonds is found in relation to his own card, this means that he is on the point of returning.

There is a variation of procedure in all the above cases, which consists in protracting the dealing till twenty-one cards have been drawn instead of fifteen. It is suggested that the predominance of red cards as the result of operation in any given instance foretells great success for the person on whose behalf the consultation is made.

Forbidden Magic Spells From The Bible

The Ace, Ten, Nine, Eight and Seven of Hearts are premonitory of news on which the Querent may be congratulated. The same cards in the suit of Clubs promise success in a lawsuit, or a lucky number in a lottery. The same in the suit of Spades portend news of a relative's death, or that of a friend, but whether there will be profit to the Querent is not so certain, having regard to the generally fatal nature of this suit, the constituents of which may be said almost to constitute the greater misfortunes in cartomancy. The particular numbers in the suit of Diamonds carry with them the same kind of prevision as Hearts.

These are but a few examples of what questions can be answered using the cards. One can create a simple spread of three cards representing the past, present and future that for most, is all that is needed to gain insight on one's future.

Another way is to only reverse the aces, as these are called the points, and are of most particular consequence; then take out the eights, for they are cards of no meaning; you will then nave twenty-eight left, which you must thus manage: shuffle them well, and deal them into four equal parcels; having first decided of what suit you will be the queen, and you must make your lover, or husband, of the same suit as yourself without regard to his complexion; take up the parcel dealt exactly before you, and then proceed regularly round to the right, examining them separately as you proceed. The first tells what is to happen soon, the second at some distance, and the third respects your husband or lover, and the fourth your secret wishes.

Forbidden Magic Spells From The Bible

Charms and Spells to Find Your True Love

ST. AGNES DAY

Falls on the 21st of January; you must prepare yourself by a twenty-four hours' fast, touching nothing but pure spring water, beginning at midnight on the 20th to the same again on the 21st; then go to bed, and mind you sleep by yourself; and do not mention what you are trying to any one, or It will break the spell; go to rest on your leftside, and repeat these lines three times:

St. Agnes be a friend to me

In the gift I ask of thee;

Let me this night my husband see -

You will now dream of your future spouse. If you see more men than one in your dream, you will wed two or three times, but, if you sleep and dream not, you will never marry.

ST. MAGDALEN

Let three young women assemble together on the eve of this saint in an upper apartment, where they are sure not to be disturbed, and let no one try whose age is more than twenty-one, or it breaks the charm; get rum, wine, gin, vinegar, and water, and let each have a hand in preparing the potion. Put it in a ground-glass vessel; no other will do. Then let each young woman dip a sprig of rosemary in, and fasten It in her bosom, and, taking three sips of the mixture, get into bed; and the three must sleep together, but not a word must be spoken after the ceremony begins, and, you will have time dreams, and of such a nature that you cannot possibly mistake your future destiny. It is not particular us to the hour in which you retire to rest.

THE CHARMS OF ST. CATHERINE

This day falls on the 25th of November, and must be thus celebrated. Let any number of young women, not exceeding seven or less than three, assemble in a room, where they are sure to be safe from interlopers; just as the clock strikes eleven at night, take from your bosom a sprig of myrtle, which you must have worn there all day, and fold it up in a bit of tissue paper, then light up a small chafing dish of charcoal, and on it let each maiden throw nine hairs from her head, and a paring of her toe and finger nails, then let each sprinkle a small quantity of myrtle and frankincense in the charcoal, and while the odoriferous vapor rises, fumigate your myrtle (this plant, or tree is consecrated to Venus) with it go to bed while the clock is striking twelve, and you will be sure to dream of your future husband, and place the myrtle exactly under your head. Observe, it is no manner of use trying this charm, if you are not a real virgin, and the myrtle hour of performance must be passed in strict silence.

HOW TO MAKE YOUR LOVER OR SWEETHEART COME TO YOU

If a maid wishes to see her lover, let her take the following method. Prick the third, or wedding finger of your left hand with a sharp needle (beware a pin), and with the blood write your own and lover's name on a piece of clean writing paper in as small a compass as you can, and encircle it with three round rings of the same crimson stream, fold it up, and at exactly the ninth hour of the evening, bury it with your hand bury it within the earth, and tell no one. Your lover will hasten to you as soon as possible, and he will not be able to rest until he sees you, and if you have quarreled, to make it up. A young man may also try this charm, only instead of the wedding finger; let him pierce his left thumb,

APPLE PARINGS

On the 28th of October, which is a double Saint's day, take an apple, pare it whole, and take the paring in your right hand, and standing in the middle of the room say the following verse:

Forbidden Magic Spells From The Bible

St. Simon and Jude,

On you I intrude,

By this paring I hold to discover,

Without any delay,

To tell me this day,

The first letter of my own true lover.

Turn round three times, and cast the paring over your left shoulder, and it will form the first letter of your future husband's surname; but if the paring breaks into many pieces, so that no letter is discernible, you will never marry; take the pips of the same apple, put them in spring water, and drink them.

TO KNOW HOW SOON A PERSON WILL BE MARRIED

Get a green pea-pod, in which are exactly nine peas, hang it over the door, and then take notice of the next person who comes in, who is not of the family, and if it proves a bachelor, you will certainly be married within that year.

On any Friday throughout the year – take rosemary flowers, bay leaves, thyme, and sweet marjoram, of each a handful; dry these and make them into a fine powder; then take a tea-spoon-fill of each sort, mix the powders together; then take twice the quantity of barley flour and make the whole into cake with the milk of a red cow.

This cake is not to be baked, but wrapped in clean writing paper, and laid under your head any Friday night. If the person dreams of music, she will wed those she desires, and that shortly; if of fire, she will be crossed in love; if of a church, she will die single. If anything is written or the least spot of ink is on the paper, it will not do.

Forbidden Magic Spells From The Bible

TO KNOW WHAT FORTUNE YOUR FUTURE HUSBAND WILL BE

Take a walnut, a hazel-nut, and nutmeg; grate them together, and mix them with butter and sugar, and make them up into small pills, of which exactly nine must be taken on going to bed; and according to her dreams, so will be the state of the person she will marry. If a gentleman, of riches; if a clergyman, of white linen; if a lawyer, of darkness; if a tradesman, of odd noises and tumults; if a soldier or sailor, of thunder and lightning; if a servant, of rain.

A CHARM FOR DREAMING

When you go to bed, place under your pillow a Common Prayer Book, open at the part of the Matrimonial service, in which is printed, "With this ring I thee wed," etc., place on a key, a ring, a flower and a sprig of willow, a small heart cake, a crust of bread, and the following cards, the ten of clubs, nine of hearts, ace of spades, and the ace of diamonds; wrap all these round in a handkerchief of thin gauze or muslin, on getting into bed cram your hoods and say:

Luna ever woman's friend,

To me thy goodness condescend;

Let me this night in visions see,

Emblems of my destiny.

If you dream of storms, trouble will betide you; if the atom ends in a fine calm, so will your fate; if of a ring, or of the act of diamonds, marriage; bread, an industrious life; cake, a prosperous life; flowers, joy; willow, treachery in love; spades, death; diamonds, money; clubs, a foreign land; hearts, illegitimate children; keys, that you will rise to great trust and power, and never know want; birds, that you will have many children, geese, that you will marry more than once.

THE FLOWER AUGURY

If a young man or woman receives a present of flowers, or a nosegay from, their sweetheart, unsolicited, for if asked for, it destroys the influence of the spell; let them keep them in the usual manner in cold water four-and-twenty hours, then shift the water, and let them stand another twenty-four hours, then take them, and immerse the stalks in water nearly boiling, leave them to perish for three hours, then look at them; if they are perished, or drooping, your lover is false; if revived and blooming, you will be happy in your choice.

HOW TO TELL BY A SCREW, WHETHER YOUR SWEETHEART LOVES YOU OR NOT

Get a small screw, such as the carpenters use for hanging closet-doors, and after making a hole in a plank with a gimlet of a proper size, put the screw in, being careful to oil the end with a little sweet oil. After having done this, take a screwdriver and drive the screw home, but you must be sure and observe how many turns it takes to get the screw in so far that it will go no farther. If it requires an odd number of turns you can rest assured that your sweetheart does not love you yet, and perhaps is enamored of some other person; but if the number of turns is an even number, be happy, for your sweetheart adores you, and lives only in the sunshine of your presence.

STRANGE BED

Lay under your pillow a prayer-book, opened at the Matrimonial Service, bound round with the garters you wore that day and a sprig of myrtle, on the page that says, "with this ring I thee wed," and your dream will be ominous, and you will have your fortune as well told as if you had paid a crown to an astrologer.

144

Forbidden Magic Spells From The Bible

A SPELL

(To be used at any convenient time)

Make a nosegay of various colored flowers, one of a sort, a sprig of rue. and some yarrow off a grave, and bind all together with the hair from your head; sprinkle them with a few drops of the oil of amber, using your left hand, and bind the flowers round your head under your night-cap when you retire to rest; put on clean sheets and linen, and your future mate will appear in your dream.

PROMISE OF MARRIAGE

If you receive a written one, or any declaration to that effect in a letter, prick the words with a sharp-pointed needle on a sheet of paper quite clear from any writing; fold in nine folds, and place it under your head when you retire to rest. If you dream of diamonds, castles, or even a clear sky, there is no deceit and you will prosper. Trees in blossom, or flowers, show children; washing, or graves, show you will lose them by death; and water shows they are faithful, but that you will go through severe poverty with the party for some time, though all may end well.

TO KNOW YOUR HUSBAND'S TRADE

Exactly at twelve, on Midsummer-day, place a bowl of water in the sun, pour in some boiling pewter as the clock is striking, saying:

Here I try a potent spell, Queen of love and Juno tell, In kind love to me, What my husband Is to be; This the day, and this the hour. When it seems you have the power or to be a maiden's friend. So, good ladies, condescend.

A tobacco-pipe full is enough. When the pewter is cold, take it out of the water, and drain it dry in a cloth, and you will find the emblems of your future husband's trade quite plain. If more than one, you will marry-twice; if confused and no emblems, you will never marry; a coach shows a gentleman for you.

Forbidden Magic Spells From The Bible

A CHRISTMAS SPELL

Steep mistletoe berries, to the number of nine, in a mixture of ale, wine, vinegar, and honey; take them on going to bed, and you will dream of your future lot; a storm in this dream is very bad; it is most likely that you will marry a sailor, who will suffer shipwreck at sea; but to see either sun, moon, or stars is an excellent presage; so are flowers; but a coffin is an unfortunate index of a disappointment in love.

THE NINE KEYS

Get nine small keys; they must all be your own by begging or purchase (borrowing will not do, nor must you tell what you want them for); plait a three-plaited braid of your own hair, and tie them together, fastening the ends with nine knots; fasten them with one of your garters to your left wrist on going to bed, and bind the other garter round your head; then say:

St. Peter take it not amiss, To try your favor I've done this; You are the ruler of the keys, Favor me, then, if you please; Let me then your influence prove, And see my dear and wedded love.

This must be done on the eve of St. Peter's. It is an old charm used by the maidens of Rome In ancient times, who put great faith in it.

THE THREE KEYS

Purchase three small keys, each at a different place, and, on going to bed, tie them together with your garter, and place them in your left hand glove, along with a small flat dough cake, on which you have pricked the first letters of your sweetheart's name; put them on your bosom when you retire to rest; if you are to have that young man, you will dream of him, but not else.

Forbidden Magic Spells From The Bible

TO KNOW IF A WOMAN WITH CHILD WILL HAVE A GIRL OR A BOY

Write the proper names of the father and the mother, and the mouth she conceived with child; count the letters in these words, and divide the amount by seven; and then, if the remainder be even, it will be a girl; if uneven, it will be a boy.

TO KNOW IF A CHILD NEW-BORN SHALL LIVE OR NOT

Write the proper names of the father and mother, and of the day the child was born; count the letters in these words, and to the amount add twenty-five, and then divide the whole by seven; if the remainder be even, the child shall die, but if it be uneven, the child shall live.

A CHARM

(To be used on the eve of any fast directed in the calendar)

This takes a week's preparation, for you must abstain from meat or strong drink. Go not to bed till the clock has struck the midnight hour, and rise before seven the next morning, the whole seven days. You must neither play at cards, or any game of chance, nor enter a place of public diversion. When you go to bed on the night of trial, eat something very salty, and do not drink after it, and you may depend on having very singular dreams; and, being very thirsty, you will probably dream of liquids. Wine is excellent, and shows wealth or promotion; brandy, foreign lands; rum, that you will wed a sailor, or one that gets his living at sea; gin, but a middling life; cordials, variety of fortune; and water, if you drink it, poverty; but to see a clear stream is good. Children are not good to behold in this dream, nor cards, nor dice; they forebode the loss of reputation, or that you will never marry.

Forbidden Magic Spells From The Bible

VALENTINE

If you receive one of those love tokens, and cannot guess at the party who sent it, the following method will explain it to a certainty. Prick the fourth finger on your left hand, and, with a crow quill, write on the back of the valentine the year, day and hour on which you were born, also the present year. Try this on the first Friday after you receive the valentine, but do not go to bed till midnight; place the paper in your left shoe, and put it under your pillow; lay on your left side, and repeat three times:

St. Valentine, pray condescend To be this night a maiden's friend; Let me now my lover see. Be he of high or low degree; By a sign his station show, Be it weal or be it woe; Let him come to my bedside, And my fortune thus decide.

The young woman will be sure to dream of the identical person who sent the valentine, and may guess, by the other particulars of the dream, if or not he is to be her spouse.

YARROW

This is a weed commonly found in abundance on graves towards the close of the spring and beginning of the summer. It must be plucked exactly on the first hour of morn; place three sprigs either in your shoe or glove, saying:

Good morning, good morning, good yarrow, And thrice a good morning to thee; Tell me before this time tomorrow Who my true love is to be.

Observe, a young man must pluck the weed off a young maiden's grave, and a female must select that of a bachelor's; retire home to bed without speaking a word, or it dissolves the spell; put the yarrow under your pillow, and it will procure a sure dream, on which you may depend.

Forbidden Magic Spells From The Bible

TO KNOW WHETHER A WOMAN SHALL HAVE THE MAN SHE WISHES

Get two lemon peels and wear them all day, one in each pocket, and at night rub the four posts of the bedstead with them; if she Is to succeed, the person will appear in her sleep, and present her with a couple of lemons; if not, there Is no hope.

TO KNOW IF ANYONE SHALL ENJOY THEIR LOVE OR NOT

Take the number of the first letter of your name, the number of the planet, and the day of the week; put all these together, and divide them by thirty; if it be above, it will come to your mind, and if below, to the contrary; and mind that number which exceeds not thirty.

SIGNS TO CHOOSE GOOD HUSBANDS AND WIVES

1. If the party be of a ruddy complexion, high and full-nosed, his eyebrows bending arch-wise, his eyes standing full, of a black and lively color, it denotes him good-natured, ingenious, and born to good fortune, and the like in a woman, if born under the planet Jupiter.

2. If the party be phlegmatic, lean, and of a dusky complexion, given much to musing and melancholy, beware of such a one, of what sex soever.

3. An indifferent wide mouth, and full cheeks, smooth forehead, little ears, dark-brown hair, and a chin proportionate to the face, is very promising.

4. An extraordinarily long chin, with the underlip larger than the upper, signifies a cross-grained person, fit for little business, yet given to folly.

5. A well-set, broad chin in a man, his face being round, and not too great, and a dimple or dent in a woman's cheek or chin denotes they will come together and live happily.

PREDICTIONS CONCERNING CHILDREN BORN ON
ANY DAY OF THE YEAR

SUNDAY-The child born on Sunday will obtain great riches, be long-lived, and enjoy much happiness.

MONDAY-Children born on this day will not be very successful in most enterprises they may engage in, being irresolute, subject to be imposed upon through their good-natured disposition; they are generally willing and ready to oblige everyone who asks a favor from them.

TUESDAY-The person born on this day will be subject to violent starts of passion, and not easily reconciled; if a man, given to illicit connections, from which conduct many serious consequences and misfortunes will arise, and lie will never be safe, being in danger of suffering death by violence, if lie does not put a restraint upon his vicious inclinations.

WEDNESDAY-The child ushered into the world on this day will be of a studious and sedate turn of mind; and if circumstances will allow, fond of perusing the literary works of the most talented ancient and modern authors. Should facilities be afforded to such a one, there is every probability of his being a highly-gifted author.

THURSDAY-Those who first see the light on this day may in general have applied to them the appellation of being "born with a silver spoon in their mouths"; for unless they resolutely spurn from them the Plutonic deity, riches will be poured into their lap with no discerning hand.

Forbidden Magic Spells From The Bible

FRIDAY-The little stranger who first inhales the vital air on this day will be blessed with a strong constitution, and will be lucky in every enterprise through life, happy in his or her domestic relations, and finally die rich and lamented.

SATURDAY-This is an unlucky day for being ushered into this world of sin and sorrow; but those born on this last day of the week may become good members of society, honored and respected by their fellow-creatures, and blessed by the Almighty.

TO DISCOVER A THIEF BY THE SIEVE AND SHEAR

Stick the points of the shears In the wood of the sieve, and let two persons support it, balanced upright, with their two fingers; then read a certain chapter in the Bible, and afterwards ask St. Peter and St. Paul if A or B is the thief, naming all the persons you suspect. On naming the real thief, the sieve will suddenly turn round about.

SIGN OF A SPEEDY MARRIAGE AND SUCCESS ATTENDING IT BY SUNDAY SIGNS

1. For a woman to have the first and last letters of her Christian name the same with the man's surname that makes love to her denotes a great union and a generous love.

2. For a man to have the first and last letters of his Christian name the same with the woman's surname denotes the some.

3. To think on a party on a sudden awaking, without any meditation, on a Friday morning that before had a place in the affection of man or woman is a demonstration of love or extraordinary friendship.

151

4. If a ring falls accidentally off a man's finger that is under no obligation of marriage and runs directly to the feet of a maid or widow, it denotes that he is not only in love with the widow, but that a sudden marriage will ensue.

5. The singing of a robin red-breast at your window, in the time of courtship, on a Wednesday, is a sign that you shall have the party desired.

6. If when walking abroad with your sweetheart, you perceive a pair of pigeons circle you round, it is a sign of marriage and happiness to ensue, with much content.

7. If a hare cross you on a Saturday morning, it promises happy days, riches, and pleasure.

ANCIENT METHODS TO KNOW THE WEATHER

In the evening when the horizon in the West is tinged with a ruddy glow, it is a sign that bright and dry weather will speedily follow.

When the sky appears ruddy in the East in the evening, changeable weather may be confidently anticipated.

Should the horizon in the North wear a ruddy appearance in the evening, stormy and boisterous weather may be expected.

When the rays from the sun at mid-day are more than ordinarily dazzling, rainy weather will shortly succeed.

In summer time, when the swallows fly near to the ground, rainy weather will assuredly soon follow.

Forbidden Magic Spells From The Bible

The shrill crowing of the cock during rainy weather is a sign that drought will speedily prevail.

When the smoke from the chimney falls down towards the ground, instead of rising upwards, it is a sign that rainy weather will soon follow.

When the face of the moon is partially obscured by a light thin vapor, rain will shortly follow.

If on a foggy morning in. summer the fog rises upwards, it will be a fine day; if the fog falls to the ground, it will be wet.

When you see the fowls in a farm-yard flocking together under some covert, be assured that ungenial weather is about to succeed.

When the rooks, on flying over your head, make an extraordinary and discordant cawing, rain will come on shortly.

When you see your dog or cat more than ordinarily restless, frisking about the house in all directions, be assured that some boisterous weather will shortly succeed.

In rainy weather, when you hear the chirping of the sparrows on the house-top more shrill than usual, it is a sign that clear and dry weather will quickly succeed.

When you see a vapory fluid resting upon a stagnant pond on the forepart of the day, you may conclude that rainy weather will shortly come on. Should the vapor ascend and clear away, a continued drought may be anticipated.

In summer, when the atmosphere is dense and heavy, and there is scarcely a breath of air, be assured that a thunderstorm is coming on.

153

Forbidden Magic Spells From The Bible

When the firmament is lighted up with meteoric phenomena, such as failing stars, globes of fire, etc., changeable and boisterous weather may be expected to prevail.

When the rising sun appears like a solid mass of fervent-heated metal, and no rays appear to emanate there from, fine and dry weather may be confidently anticipated.

When the sun sets in a halo of ruddy brightness, genial and bright weather may be fully relied on for the coming day.

When the moon appears of a ruddy hue, stormy and boisterous weather may be expected to follow.

When the stars appear of a sparkling brightness, fine and genial weather may be expected to prevail for some time. Should the stars appear obscure and dim, changeable and rainy weather may be anticipated.

When, in summer time, yon see the cattle grazing in a field gathering together in groups, be assured that a thunder-storm is approaching.

The luminous appearance of the Aurora Borealis, or Northern Lights, foretells the approach of stormy and boisterous weather.

When the Betting sun in the autumn or winter seasons appears ruddy, it is a sign that high and boisterous winds may be expected to blow from, the North and Northwest. When the sun at its rising in the autumn or winter seasons appears ruddy, it foretells that high and boisterous winds may be anticipated to blow from the South and Southeast

When the sea-birds are observed flocking towards the shore, storms and tempests may be confidently expected.

When, in the early autumn season, the migratory birds are seen flocking together, and raking their departure, it is a certain sign that rough and boisterous weather is approaching, and that a severe winter may be anticipated.

When the doves around a dove-cote make a more than ordinary cooing, and frequently pass in and out of their cote, it is a sign that a change of weather is near.

When the robin approaches your habitation, it is a sign that wintry weather will shortly prevail.

When there is a thick vapory mist resting on the tops of high hills in the morning, and remains there during the day, it is a sign that wet and ungenial weather may be anticipated, should the mist eventually rise upward, and be evaporated by the sun's rays, a return to fine, dry weather may be looked for; if, how-aver, the mist falls down into the valley, a continuation of wet weather will prevail.

SIGNS AND OMENS: AUGURIES AND FOREWARNINGS

However skeptical some persons may pro fess to be on the subject of signs, auguries, and forewarnings, still few will venture to deny that in innumerable instances those mysterious admonitions and forewarnings have been speedily followed by events of a pleasant or a painful nature to those who have received them. The belief in signs and auguries has been cherished by mankind ever since the creation; and this faculty is not confined to the human family alone, but the lower animals possess some of them in an extraordinary degree. The following are a few of the multifarious signs and auguries which admonish and forewarn mankind, at one time or another:

Should you be the subject of a deep depression of spirits, contrary to your usual constitutional buoyancy and liveliness, it is a sign that you are about to receive some agreeable intelligence.

Forbidden Magic Spells From The Bible

If the crown of your head itches more than ordinary, you may expect to be advanced to a more honorable position in life. Should the hair on your head come off, when combing, in greater quantities than usual, it is a sign that you will soon be the subject of a severe attack of affliction.

If your right eyebrow should immoderately itch, be assured that you are going to look upon a pleasant sight - a long-absent friend, or a long-estranged, but now reconciled, lover.

Should your left eyebrow be visited with a tantalizing itching, it is a sign that you will soon look upon a painful sight – the corpse of a valued friend, or your lover walking with a favored rival.

A ringing in your right ear is an augury that you will shortly hear some pleasant news.

A ringing in your left ear is a sign that you will in a short time receive intelligence of a very unpleasant nature. When your left ear tingles some one is back-biting you.

A violent itching of the nose foretells trouble and sorrow to those who experience it.

An itching of the lips in a sign that someone is speaking disrespectfully of you.

When you are affected by an itching on the back of your neck, be assured that either yourself or someone nearly related to you is about to suffer a violent death.

An itching on the right shoulder signifies that you will shortly have a large legacy bequeathed to you.

Forbidden Magic Spells From The Bible

When you feel an itching sensation on your left shoulder, be sure that you are about to bear a heavy burden of sorrow and trouble.

If your right elbow joint itches, you may expect shortly to hear some intelligence that will give you extreme pleasure.

Should you be annoyed with a violent itching on your left elbow joint, you may be sure that some vexatious disappointment will be experienced by you,

If you feel an itching on the palm of your right hand, you may expect soon to receive some money which you have been long expecting.

When the palm of your left hand itches, you may expect to be called upon to pay some money for a debt which you have not personally incurred.

An itching on the spine of your back is a sign that you will shortly be called upon to bear a heavy burden of sorrow and trouble.

An itching on your loins is an indication that you will soon receive an addition to your family, if married; if single, that you are on the eve of marriage.

When you are affected with an itching on the belly; expect to be invited to feast upon a choice collection of savory meats.

When either or both of your thighs itch, be assured that you are about to change your sleeping apartment.

If you have an itching sensation in your right knee, depend upon it that you will shortly undergo a remarkable and beneficial change in your previous course of life, and become religiously inclined.

Forbidden Magic Spells From The Bible

If a similar sensation prevails in your right knee, you may expect to undergo a change in your deportment of an unfavorable nature.

An itching sensation on the shins foretells that you will be visited with a painful and long-continued affliction.

When your ankle-joints itch, be sure that you are about to be united to one whom you love, if single; if married, that your domestic comforts will be largely increased.

When the sole of your right foot itches, you may feel assured that you are about to undertake a journey from which you will derive much pleasure and enjoyment.

Should you experience a similar sensation on the sole of your left foot, you may expect to be called upon to take a journey of an unpleasant and melancholy nature.

If, in taking a walk, you should see a single magpie, it is a bad omen, especially if it should fly past you to the left hand; but if it should pass you to the right hand, the good will counterbalance the bad. Should you see two magpies together, expect to hear of something to your advantage – a proposal of marriage, if single; or a legacy of money bequeathed to you. Should the magpies fly past you together to your right hand, your own marriage, or the marriage of someone nearly related to you, will occur in a short time. The seeing of several magpies together is considered a very fortunate omen.

May is considered an unlucky month to marry in; therefore avoid doing so if possible. If you can catch a snail by the horns on the first of May, and throw it over your shoulders, you will be lucky throughout the year. If you place one on a slate on that day, it will describe by its turnings the initials of your future partner's name.

Forbidden Magic Spells From The Bible

If a young man or young woman, on going up a flight of stairs, should stumble in the middle of the flight, it is a sign that his or her marriage will take place in a short time. If the stumbling should be near the top of the stairs, then his or her marriage will be immediately consummated.

If a young person, when seated at the tea-table, should observe one or more stalks of the tea-plant in the newly-poured-out cup, and if, on stirring the tea and holding the spoon in the middle of the liquid, the stalk or stalks should come close to the spoon handle, it is a token that he or she will be soon married.

When the house-dog is unusually restless, and howls dismally in the night-time, it is a sign that sickness and death are about to visit the family to whom the dog belongs.

When the wick of your candle shows a bright spark in the midst of the flame, it is a sign that a long-absent friend is about to visit you.

When the ribs of your fire-grate are more than usually covered with flukes of soot, it is a sign that a stranger is about to visit your habitation.

If a person stumbles when leaving his house at the beginning of a journey, or trips or stumbles more than once during the course of the journey, it is advisable to postpone it.

It is bad luck to sweep the kitchen floor after dark, and you are sweeping out good luck if you sweep dirt out the door.

If you burn beef bones by mistake it is a sign of much sorrow to come on account of poverty. To burn fish or poultry bones indicates that scandal will be spread about you.

Forbidden Magic Spells From The Bible

To cross two forks accidentally is a sign that slander will be spread about you. To stir anything with a fork is to stir up misfortune. As well, crossing two table-knives by accident portends bad luck.

To be completely naked in your dream is a very lucky omen. If only your feet are bare, you will have many difficulties to overcome before you can reach your goal. Also, to dream of someone smoking a cigar indicates that money is on its way.

If you involuntarily make a rhyme, that is a lucky omen. Before speaking again, make a wish, and the chances are that it will come true.

It is a sign of good luck if you first see the new moon over your left shoulder, but of bad luck if you see it over your right. Should you have money in your pocket at the time of the new moon, you will be penniless before the moon is in the full.

To sneeze three times in rapid succession is considered by some to be a good omen.

It is a sure sign that your plans will meet with success if three bees alight on you at the same time.

If you find a coin, you should spit on it to bring good luck.

If the palm of the left hand itches you will be getting money; if the right palm itches, you will be losing/spending money.

A dog passing between a couple about to be married means ill fortune will befall the couple. However, being followed by a strange dog indicates good luck.

FORTUNE TELLING WITH TEA OR COFFEE

Pour the grounds of tea or coffee into a white cup; shake them well about, so as to spread them over the surface; reverse the cop to drain away the superfluous contents, and then exercise jour fertile fancy in discovering what the figures thus formed represent Long, wavy lines denote vexatious and losses-their importance depending on the number of lines. Straight ones, on the contrary, foretell peace, tranquility, and long life.

Human figures are usually good omens, announcing love affairs, and marriage.

If circular figures predominate, the person for whom the experiment is made may expect to receive money. If these circles are connected by straight, unbroken lines, there will be delay, but ultimately all will be satisfactory, Squares, foretell peace and happiness; oblong figures, family discord; whilst curved, twisted, or angular ones, are certain signs of vexations and annoyances, their probable duration being determined by the number of figures.

A crown signifies honor; a cross, news of death; a ring, marriage-if a letter can be discovered near it that will be the initial of the name of the future spouse. If the ring is in the clear part of the cup, it foretells happy union; if clouds are about it, the contrary; but if it should chance to be quite at the bottom, then the marriage will never take place.

A leaf of clover, or trefoil, is a good sign, denoting, if at the top of the cup, speedy good fortune, which will be more or less distant in case it appears at, or Dear the bottom.

The anchor, if at the bottom of the cup, denotes success in business; at the top, and in the clear part, love and fidelity; but in thick, or cloudy parts, inconstancy.

The serpent is always the sign of an enemy, and if in the cloudy part, gives warning that great prudence will be necessary to ward off misfortune.

161

Forbidden Magic Spells From The Bible

The coffin portends news of a death, or long illness.

The dog, at the top of the cup, denotes true and faithful friends; in the middle, that they are not to be trusted; but at the bottom, that they are secret enemies.

The lily, at the top of the cup, foretells a happy marriage; at the bottom, anger.

A letter signifies news; if in the dear, very welcome ones; surrounded by dots, a remittance of money; but if hemmed in by clouds, bad tidings, and losses. A heart near it denotes a love letter. A single portends restoration to health; a group of trees in the dear; misfortunes, which may be avoided; several trees, wide apart, promise that your wishes 'will be accomplished; if encompassed by dashes, it is a token that your fortune is in its blossom, and only requires care to bring to maturity; if surrounded by dots, riches.

Mountains signify either friends or enemies, according to their situation.

The sun, moon, and stars, denote happiness, success. The clouds, happiness or misfortune, according as they are bright or dark.

Birds are good omens, but quadrupeds-with the exception of the dog-foretell trouble and difficulties.

Fish; imply good news from across the water.

A triangle portends an unexpected legacy; a single straight line, a journey.

The figure of a man, indicates a speedy visitor; if the arm is outstretched, a present; when the figure is very distinct, it shows that the person expected will be of dark complexion, and vice versa.

A crown, near a cross, indicates a large fortune, resulting from a death.

Flowers are signs of joy, happiness, and peaceful life.

A heart, surrounded by dots, signifies joy, occasioned by the receipt of money; with a ring near it, approaching marriage.

HOW TO READ YOUR FORTUNE BY THE WHITE OF AN EGG

Break a new-laid egg, and, carefully separating the yolk from the white, drop the latter into a large tumbler half full of water; place this, uncovered, in some dry place, and let it remain untouched for four-and-twenty hours, by which time the white of the egg will have formed itself into various figures-rounds, squares, ovals, animals, trees, crosses, which are to be interpreted in the same manner as those formed by the coffee grounds. Of course, the more whites there are in the glass, the more figures there will be.

This is a very interesting experiment, and much practiced by the young Scotch maidens, who, however, believe it to have more efficacies when tried on either Midsummer Eve or Halloween.

USING AN EGG TO REMOVE BAD LUCK

If you are plagued by evil spells and bad luck, try this powerful, ancient spell to help you remove any bewitchment from your life.

You must purchase a brown fresh egg before noon of that day. Make sure that you start this when the moon is waning. It is very important that this egg be fresh. Place this egg in a brown bag and tie the neck of the bag with a black cloth string. Place this bag under your bed.

Each night before retiring to bed, you must open this bag and take the egg out and rub it all over your body. When done, put the egg back into the bag, take a deep breath and blow three times into the bag. When you are blowing into the bag, you must imagine that all the bad luck is leaving your body through your breath.

When done, place the bag back under your bed. Do this for nine days. At the end of nine days, take the bag with the egg and dispose of it outside your home.

Each time that you blow into the bag, you must immediately tie it back up. If by the end of seven days you notice that your bag is moving on its own. Stop, and dispose of the bag immediately. Do not look into the bag and make sure that the bag is secure. Only do this if you are serious about removing bad luck and evil bewitchments in your life.

HOW TO TELL FORTUNES BY THE MOLES ON A PERSON'S BODY

1. A mole that stands on the right side of the forehead, or tight temple, signifies that the person will arrive to sudden wealth and honor.

2. A mole on the right eyebrow, announces speedy marriage, the husband to possess many good qualities and a large fortune.

3. A mole on the left of either of those three places, portends unexpected disappointment in your most sanguine wishes.

4. A mole on the outside of either eye, denotes the person to be of a steady, sober, and sedate disposition.

5. A mole on either cheek, signifies that the person never shall rise above mediocrity in point of fortune.

6. A mole on the nose, shows that the person will have good success in his or her undertakings.

Forbidden Magic Spells From The Bible

7. A mole on the lip, either upper or lower, proves the person to be fond of delicate things, and much given to the pleasures of love, in which he or she will most commonly be successful.

8. A mole on the chin, indicates that the person will be attended with great prosperity, and be highly esteemed.

9. A mole on the side of the neck, shows that the person will narrowly escape suffocation; but will afterward rise to great consideration by an unexpected legacy or inheritance.

10. A mole on the throat, denotes that the person shall become rich, by marriage.

11. A mole on the right breast, declares the person to be exposed to a sudden reverse from comfort to distress, by unavoidable accidents. Most of his children will be girls.

12. A mole on the left breast, signifies success in undertakings and an amorous disposition. Most of his children will be boys.

13. A mole on the bosom, portends mediocrity of health and fortune.

14. A mole under the left breast, over the heart, foreshows that a man will be of a warm disposition, unsettled in mind, fond of rambling, and light in his conduct. In a lady it shows sincerity in love, and easy travail in child-birth.

15. A mole on the right side over any part of the ribs, denotes the person to be pusillanimous, and slow in understanding anything that may be attended with difficulties.

16. A mole on the belly, shows the person to be addicted to sloth and gluttony, and not very choice in point of dress.

17. A mole on either hip, shows that the person will have many children, and that they will be healthy and possess much patience.

18. A mole on the right thigh, is an indication of riches, and much happiness in the married state.

19. A mole on the left thigh, denotes poverty and want of friends through the enmity and injustice of others.

20. A mole on the right knee, shows the person will be fortunate In the choice of a partner for life, and meet with few disappointments in the world.

21. A mole on the left knee, portends that the person will be rash, inconsiderate, and hasty, but modest when in cool blood.

22. A mole on either leg, shows that the person is indolent, thoughtless, and indifferent as to whatever may happen.

23. A mole on either ankle, denotes a man to be inclined to effeminacy and elegance of dress; a lady to be courageous, active and industrious, with a trifle of the termagant.

24. A mole on either foot, forebodes sudden illness or unexpected misfortune.

25. A mole on the right shoulder, indicates prudence, discretion, secrecy, and wisdom.

26. A mole on the left shoulder, declares a testy, contentious, and ungovernable spirit.

27. A mole on the right arm, denotes vigor and courage.

28. A mole on the left arm, declares resolution and victory in battle.

29. A mole near either elbow, denotes restlessness, a roving and unsteady temper, also a discontentedness with those which they are obliged to live constantly with.

30. A mole between the elbow and the wrist, promises the person prosperity, but not until he has undergone many hardships.

31. A mole on the wrist, or between it, and the ends of the fingers, shows industry, parsimony, and conjugal affection.

32. A mole on any part, from the shoulders to the loins, is indicative of imperceptible decline and gradual decay, whether of health or wealth.

LIST OF UNLUCKY DAYS, WHICH, TO ANYONE BORN ON THEM, WILL GENERALLY PROVE UNFORTUNATE

January 6, 6, 13, 14, 20, and 21.

February 2, 3, 9, 10, 16, 17, 22, and 23.

March I, 2, 8, 9, 16, 17, 28, and 29.

April 24 and 25,

May 1, 2, 9, 17, 22, 29, and 30.

June 5, 6, 12, 13, 18, and 19

July 3 and 4.

Forbidden Magic Spells From The Bible

September 9 and 16.

October 20 and 27.

November 9, 10, 21, 29, and 30

December 6, 14, and 21.

I particularly advise anyone born on these days to be extremely cautious of placing their affections too hastily, as they will be subject to disappointments and vexations in that respect; it will be better for them (in those matters) to be guided by the advice of their friends, rather than by their own feelings, they will be less fortunate in placing their affections, than in any other action of their lives, as many of these marriages will terminate in separations, divorces, etc.

My readers must be well aware that affairs of importance begun at inauspicious times, by those who have been born at those periods when the stars shed their malign influence, can seldom, if ever, lead to much good: it is, therefore, that I endeavor to lay before them a correct statement drawn from accurate astrological information, in order that by strict attention and care, they may avoid falling into those perplexing labyrinths from which nothing but that care and attention can save them.

The list of days I have above given will be productive of hasty and clandestine marriages – marriages under untoward circumstances, perplexing attachments, and, as a natural consequence, the displeasure of friends, together with family dissensions, and division.

LIST OF DAYS USUALLY CONSIDERED FORTUNATE

With respect to Courtship, Marriage and Love affairs in general - females that were born on the following days may expect Court ships and prospects of Marriage which will have a happy termination.

January 1, 2, 15, 26, 27, 28.

February 11, 21, 26, 26.

March 10, 24.

April 6, 15, 16, 20, 28.

May 3, 13, 18, 31.

June 10, 11, 15, 22, 25.

July 9, 14, 15, 28.

August 6, 7, 10, 11, 16, 20, 25.

September 4, 8, 9, 17, 18, 23.

October 3, 7, 16, 21, 22.

November 5, 14, 20.

December 14, 15, 19, 20, 22, 23, 25.

Although the greater number, or indeed nearly all the ladies that are born on the days stated in the preceding list, will be likely to meet with a prospect of marriage, or become engaged in some love affair of more than ordinary importance, yet it must not be expected that the result will be the same with all of them; with some they will terminate in marriage with others in disappointment and some of them will be in danger of forming attachments that may prove of a somewhat troublesome description.

I shall, therefore, in order to enable my readers to distinguish them, give a comprehensive and useful list, showing which of them will be most likely to marry. Those born within the limits of the succeeding List of Hours, on any of the preceding days, will be the most likely to marry or win, at least, have Courtships that will be likely to have a happy termination.

THE MOON - JUDGMENTS DRAWN FROM THE MOON'S AGE

1. A child born within twenty-four hours after the new moon will be fortunate and live to a good old ace. Whatever is dreamt on that day will be fortunate and pleasing to the dreamer.

2. The second day is very lucky for discovering things lost, or hidden treasure; the child born on this day shall thrive.

Forbidden Magic Spells From The Bible

3. The child born on the third day will be fortunate through persons in power, and whatever is dreamed will prove true.

4. The fourth day is bad; persons falling sick on this day rarely recover.

5. The fifth day is favorable to begin a good work, and the dreams will be tolerably successful; the child born on this day will be vain and deceitful.

6. The sixth day the dreams will not immediately come to pass and the child born will not live long.

7. On the seventh day do not tell your dreams, for much depends on concealing them; if sickness befalls you on this day, you will soon recover; the child born will live long, but have many troubles.

8. On the eighth day the dreams will come to pass; whatever business a person undertakes on this day will prosper.

9. The ninth day differs very little from the former; the child born on this day will arrive at great riches and honor.

10. The tenth day is likely to be fatal; those who fall sick will rarely recover, but the 2bild born on this day will live long and be a great traveler.

11.   The child that is born on the eleventh day will be much devoted to religion and have an engaging form and manners.

12. On the twelfth day the dreams are rather fortunate, and the child burn shall live long.

13. On the thirteenth day the dreams will prove true in a very short time.

14. If you ask a favor of any one on the fourteenth day, it will be granted.

15. The sickness that befalls a person on the fifteenth day is likely to prove mortal.

16. The child that is born on the sixteenth day will be of very ill-manners and unfortunate; it is nevertheless a good day for the buying and selling of all kinds of merchandise.

17. The child born on the seventeenth day will be very foolish; it is a very unfortunate day to transact any kind of business, or contract marriage.

18. The child born on the eighteenth day will be vigilant, but will suffer considerable hardships; if a female, she will be chaste and industrious, and live respected to n great age.

19. The nineteenth day is dangerous; the child born will be very ill-disposed and malicious.

20. On the twentieth day the dreams are true, but the child born will be dishonest.

21. The child born on the twenty-first day will grow up healthy and strong, but be of a very selfish, ungenteel turn of mind.

22. The child born on the twenty-second day will be fortunate; he or she will be of a cheerful countenance, religious, and much be loved.

23. The child that is born on the twenty-third day will be of an ungovernable temper, will forsake his friends, and choose to wander about in a foreign country, and will be very unhappy through life.

24. The child born on the twenty-fourth day will achieve many heroic actions, and will be much admired for his extraordinary abilities.

25. The child born on the twenty-fifth day will be very wicked; he will meet with many dangers, and is likely to come to an ill end.

26. On the twenty-sixth day the dreams are certain - the child then born will be rich, and much esteemed.

27. The twenty-seventh day is very favorable for dreams, and the child then born will be of a sweet and humble disposition.

28. The child born the twenty-eighth day will be the delight of his parents, but will not live to any great age.

29. Children born on the twenty-ninth day will experience many hardships, though in the end they may turn out happily. It is good to marry on this day; and business begun on this day will be prosperous.

30. The child that is born on the thirtieth day will be fortunate and happy, and well skilled in the arts and sciences.

TO CAST YOUR NATIVITY

Having ascertained the exact time of your birth, and the hour in which you entered this transitory life, procure a Moore's almanac of that year, which will direct you to the sign that then reigned, the name of the planets, and the state of the moon; particularly observe whether the sun was just entering the sign, whether it was near the end, or what was its particular progress; if at the beginning, your fate will be strongly tinctured with its properties, moderate at the meridian, and slightly if the sun is nearly going out of the Write down the day of the week; see whether it is a lucky day or not, the state of the moon, the nature of the planets, and the influence described next, and you will ascertain your future destiny with very little trouble.

JANUARY

(Aquarius or the Water Bearer.)

Gives a love of wandering and variety, seldom contented long in one place; soon affronted, and slow to forgive; fond of law, though they lose the day. They are unhappy. Mercury gives them slights in love. A full moon is the best, for a new moon only adds to their false fears; and Saturn gives them real trouble to content with.

FEBRUARY

(Pisces, or the Fishes.)

Those born under the influence of this planet prosper beat on the ocean, or at a distance from their native home. But those born under this sign, and not ordained to travel, will experience at times more or less distress. Mars and Jupiter are the best planets, and if the day of the week on which they, were born be a fortunate one, let them begin their fresh concerns on that day, write and answer letters, or seek for money due to them according to their rule, and they have more than a chance for prosperity. The female traveler will be very fortunate, and have a contempt for danger, yet neither her disposition nor manners will be masculine; she will make an excellent wife and mother, and, if left a widow with children, will strive for their interest with a father's care and prudence; nor will she wed a second time, unless Venus rules her destiny, liars give her success; Jupiter, vigilance; a new moon, virtue; a full moon, some enemies; and Saturn, temptation; yet she will prosper.

Forbidden Magic Spells From The Bible

MARCH

(Aries, or the Ram.)

A very good sign to those born under it To either sex denotes prosperity, fidelity, dutiful children, and many liberal friends, but hot-tempered; if Mercury Is one of the planets, they will then be very amiable. Jupiter and Venus are also good planets to them, but Mars or Saturn causes a sad alteration to their general destiny, and gives a mixed life of wine and pleasure. Venus reigning alone as a morning star at the time of their birth causes them many amours.

APRIL

(Taurus, or the Bull.)

To be prosperous under this sign will require active industry and patience under misfortunes and perils; but Jupiter, Venus, or the new moon, will soften this destiny. The men will be bold and adventurous, fond of governing, and hard to please; they must be careful not to enter on any fresh concern while their sign has the ascendancy, the end of April and the tw6 first weeks in May.

MAY

(Gemini, or the Twins) Very fortunate for females, particularly in the grand article of matrimony, though they will prosper well in other affairs; the full moon and Venus are good for them. They will be punctual and honest in their dealings, be much respected by their friends and neighbors, and have many children.

JUNE

(Cancer, or the Crab)

A prosperous but eventful sign to both sexes, but more particularly those of a fair complexion; they will be exalted in life; Jupiter and Venus are the best signs for them; but the brunettes, though fortunate, will plague themselves and others with whims, curiosities, and ill-nature, and may be particular about mere trifles. If Man be their planet, they will enter into lawsuits; and if Saturn; let them beware of ungovernable passions.

Forbidden Magic Spells From The Bible

JULY

(Leo, or the Lion)

Favorable to those born in poverty, but not to the rich; for this sign always shows a great change of circumstances about the meridian of our days, sooner or later, according to the sign in which you were born. If Jupiter be the planet, the person born poor will become rich by legacies, or will probably marry their master or mistress, or his or her son or daughter, according to their sex, and lead a happy life. This has often proved true.

AUGUST

(Virgo, or the Virgin)

A most important sign; the men brave, generous, candid, and honest; the females amicable and prosperous, If they do not mar their own fortune by love of flattery, to which they will be prone, or else advancement awaits them. Venus is not a good planet for them, and Saturn shows seduction; but, if neither of these three planets predominate at the time of their birth, they will marry early, have good children, and enjoy the most valuable blessings of life, and have many unexpected gains.

SEPTEMBER

(Libra, or the Balance)

A middle course of life is promised by this sign; a smooth, even, unrippled stream, free from storms or sudden changes; in fact, an enviable destiny. The persons now born will be just in their transactions, faithful in love and wedlock, and averse to litigation and law; not many children, but those healthy.

OCTOBER

(Scorpio, or the Scorpion)

To the man, promises a long, active, useful life, and an intelligent mind; prosperous and very careful of what he gains; a good husband, parent and master, and a sincere friend; a little gay in his youthful days, but not vicious. Jupiter and a full moon add to the good of his destiny; Saturn or Mercury will detract from it; Venus inclines him to the fair sex. To the woman this sign shows indolence; and, if she is well off in the world, it will not be by her own merit or industry, for she will have to thank those to whom it is her good fortune to be nearly allied; but, If she has no shining qualities that are prominent, she will be free from evil propensities, and will never bring disgrace on herself, her husband, her family, or friends, unless Venus reigned at her birth; then I fear for her; but no other planet will affect her destiny.

NOVEMBER

(Sagittarius, or the Archer)

Gives to both sexes an amorous disposition, and if Venus or Mercury presides at their birth, they will love variety; out Jupiter and Mars are good for them; the new moon is excellent to the female, add full to the man. It is seldom that persons born in this sign marry, if the first-mentioned planets reign; or, if they do marry, it is late in life, or when the meridian of their days are over, and they are become wise enough to relinquish folly; they then become steady and prudent, and generally do well; they seldom have many children, but what they have will prosper, and have friends who will promote their interest.

DECEMBER

(Capricorn, or the Goat)

Shows you will work and toil, and others reap the benefit of your labor, unless marriage) alters the destiny; out hard will be your fate if your spouse is of the same sign as yourself; but. If Jupiter be one of the planets at your birth, the end of your days will be more prosperous than the beginning, after experiencing many cares and obstructions. A woman may probably better her fate by a second marriage, especially if Venus be her planet.

LOVE PRESENTS AND WITCHING SPELLS

Take three hairs from your head, roll them up in a small compact form, and anoint them with three drops of blood from the left-hand fourth finger, choosing tills because the anatomists say a vein goes from that finger to the heart; wear this In your bosom (taking care that none knows the secret) for nine days and nights; then enclose the hair in the secret cavity of a ring or a brooch, and present it to your lover. While it is in his possession, it will have the effect of preserving his love, and leading his mind to dwell on you.

A chain or plait of your own hair, mixed with that of a goat, and anointed with nine drops of the essence of ambergris, will have a similar effect.

Flowers prepared with your own blood will have an effect on your lover's mind; but the impression will be very transient, and fade with the flowers. If your love should be fortunate, and you are married to the object of your wishes, never reveal to him the nature of the present you made him, or it may have the fatal effect of turning love into hate.

DREAMS - How to Receive Oracles by Dreams

He who would receive true dreams, should keep a pure, undisturbed, and imaginative spirit, and so compose it that it may be made worthy of knowledge and government by the mind; for such a spirit is most fit for prophesying, and is a most clear glass of all images which flow everywhere from all things. When, therefore, we are sound in body, not disturbed in mind, our intellect not made dull by heavy meats and strong drink, not sad through poverty, not provoked through lust, not incited by any vice, nor stirred up by wrath or anger, not being irreligiously and profanely inclined, not given to levity nor lost to drunkenness, but, chastely going to bed, fall asleep, then our pure and divine soul being free from all the evils above recited, and separated from all hurtful thoughts-and now freed, by dreaming is endowed with this divine spirit as an instrument, and doth receive those beams and representations which are darted down, as it were, and shine forth from, the divine Hind into itself, in a deifying glass.

There are four kinds of true dreams, viz., the first, matutine, i.e., between sleeping and waking; the second, that which one sees concerning another; the third, that whose interpretation is shown to the same dreamer in the nocturnal vision; and, lastly, that which-is related to the same dreamer in the nocturnal vision. But natural things and their own co-mixtures do likewise belong unto wise men, and we often use such to receive oracles from a spirit by a dream, which are either by perfumes, unctions, meats, drinks, rings, seals, etc.

Now those who are desirous to receive oracles through a dream, let them make themselves a ring of the Sun or Saturn for this purpose. There are likewise images of dreams, which, being put under the head when going to sleep, doth effectually give true dreams of whatever the mind hath before determined or consulted upon, the practice of which is as follows:

Thou Shalt make an image of the Sun, the figure whereof must be a man sleeping upon the bosom of an angel; which thou shall make when Leo ascends, the Sun being in the ninth house in Aries; then you must write upon the figure the name of the effect desired, and in the hand of the angel the name and character of the intelligence of the Sun, which is Michael.

Let the same Image be made in Virgo ascending--Mercury being fortunate in Aries in the ninth, or Gemini ascending, Mercury being fortunate in the ninth house in Aquarius and let him be received by Saturn with a fortunate aspect, and let the name of the spirit (which is Raphael) be written upon it. Let the same likewise be made-Libra ascending, Venus being received from Mercury in Gemini in the ninth house-and write upon it the name of the angel of Venus (which is Anacl). Again you may make the same image-Aquarius ascending, Saturn fortunately possessing the ninth in his exaltation, which is Libra-and let there be written upon it the name of the angel of Saturn (which is Cassial). The same may be made with Cancer ascending, the Moon being received by Jupiter and Venus in Pisces, and being fortunately placed in the ninth house-and write upon it the spirit of the Moon (which is Gabriel).

There are likewise made rings of dreams of wonderful efficacy, and there are rings of the Sun and Saturn-and the constellation of them in, when the Sun or Saturn ascend in their exaltation in the ninth, and when the Moon is joined to Saturn in the ninth, and in that sign which was the ninth house of the nativity, and write and engrave upon the rings the name of the spirit of the Sun or Saturn; and by these rules you may know how and by what means to constitute more of yourself.

But know this, that such images work nothing (as they are simply images), except they are vivified by spiritual and celestial virtue, and chiefly by the ardent desire and firm intent of the soul of the operator. But who can give a soul to an image, or make a stone, or metal, or clay, or wood, or wax, or paper, to live? Certainly no man whatever; for this arcanum doth not enter into an artist of a stiff neck. He only hath it who transcends the progress of angels, and comes to the very Archtype Himself. The tables of numbers likewise confer to the receiving of oracles, being duly formed under their own constellations.

Therefore, he who is desirous of receiving true oracles by dreams, let him abstain from supper, from drink, and be otherwise well disposed, so his brain will be free from turbulent vapors; let him also have his bed-chamber fair and clean, exorcised and consecrated; then let him perfume the same with some convenient fumigation, and let him anoint his temples with some unguent efficacious hereunto, and put a ring of dreams upon his finger; then let him take one of the images we have spoken of, and place the same under his head; then let him address himself to sleep, meditating upon that thing which he desires to know. So shall he receive a most certain and undoubted oracle by a dream when the Moon goes through the sign of the ninth revolution of his nativity, and when she is in the ninth sign from the sign of perfection.

This is the way whereby we may obtain all sciences and arts whatsoever, whether astrology, occult philosophy, physic, etc. or else suddenly and perfectly with a true Illumination of our Intellect, although all inferior familiar spirits whatsoever conduce to this effect, and sometimes also evil spirits sensibly inform us, intrinsically and extrinsically.

FINGER-NAIL OBSERVATIONS

Broad nails show the person to be bashful, fearful, but of gentle nature.

When there is a certain white mark at the extremity of them, it shows that the person has more honesty than subtlety, and that his worldly substance will be impaired through negligence.

Long white nails denote much sickness and infirmity, especially fevers, an indication of strength and deceit by women. If upon the white anything appears at the extremity that is pale, it denotes short life by sudden death, and the person to be given to melancholy.

Forbidden Magic Spells From The Bible

When there appears a certain mixed redness, of colors, at the beginning of the nails, it shows the person to be choleric and quarrelsome.

When the extremity is black it is a sign of husbandry.

Narrow nails denote the person to be inclined to mischief and to do injury to his neighbor.

Long nails show the person to be good-natured, but mistrustful, and loves reconciliation rather than differences.

Oblique nails signify deceit and want of courage, little and round nails denote obstinate anger and hatred. If they be crooked at the extremity, they show pride and fierceness.

Round nails show a choleric person, yet soon reconciled, honest, and a lover of secret sciences.

Fleshy nails denote the person to be mild in his temper, idle, and lazy pale and black nails show the person to he very deceitful to his neighbor, and subject to many diseases.

Red and marked nails signify a choleric and martial nature, given to cruelty; and, as many little marks aft there are, they speak of so many evil desires.

TRADITIONAL WAY TO BAFFLE YOUR ENEMIES

Repeat reverently, and with sincere faith, the following words, and you will be protected in the hour of danger:

"Behold, God is my salvation; I will trust, and not be afraid, for the Lord Jehovah is my strength and my song; he also is become my salvation.

"For the stars of heaven, and the constellation thereof, shall not give their light; the sun shall be darkened in his going forth, and the moon shall not cause her tight to shine.

"And behold, at eventide, trouble; and before morning he is not; this is the portion of them that spoil us, and the lot of them that rob us."

CHARM AGAINST TROUBLE IN GENERAL

Repeat reverently, and with sincere faith, the following words, and you shall be protected in the hour of danger:

"He shall deliver thee in six troubles, yea, in seven there shall no evil touch thee; in famine he shall redeem thee from death, and in war from the power of the sword; and thou shall know that thy tabernacle shall be in peace, and thou shalt visit thy habitation and shall not err."

Forbidden Magic Spells From The Bible

VIV. How To Create Your Own Bible Magic

THE LINE that separates magic from religion is extremely tenuous. Scripture is sacred not only for the wisdom it teaches, but even more for its close association with the person of the deity who revealed it. It speaks in the voice of God, and therefore it possesses something of the personality and attributes of deity. Because of this schools of mystical and esoteric exegesis emerged which profess to discover the hidden inner significance of the Word.

Many ancient books of wisdom were once pressed into service for magical purposes. The words of holy writ were considered to be potent charms against the forces of evil. During special circumstances when spirit attacks were feared, such as prior to a funeral, the night before circumcision (the Wachnacht), the eight nights after birth, or the nights of holy days, studying the Bible and other holy writings was a common practice. "As soon as a man has ceased his preoccupation with the words of Torah Satan has permission to attack."

The use of "words of Torah" for specific magical purposes goes back to antiquity. The injunction of Deut. 6:9, "And thou shalt write them upon the doorposts of thy house and upon thy gates," whether originally meant altogether literally or not, was so understood, and the mezuzah from earliest times until today has been looked upon as an amulet to protect the home against demons.

The use of Biblical verses as charms was not unknown in the Talmudic period. If one dreamt of a stream, he was advised to recite Is. 66:12, "I will extend peace to her like a river" immediately upon waking, lest the words "distress will come in like a flood" (Is. 59:19) occur to him first; Ps. 29:3-10, containing seven references to "the voice of God," was suggested to protect one who must drink water on a night when the evil spirits are particularly active; the words of Nu. 23:22-23, beginning with "El" (God) and ending with "El," ward off the ill effect that resulted from a dog or a woman passing between two men.

A sixteenth-century authority, R. Hayim b. Bezalel, attempted to negate the obvious sense of such devices: "The Talmud advises us," he wrote, "that when a man recites the sentences beginning and ending with 'El' he cannot be harmed by any enchantment or sorcery; the point of this is that the man who believes wholeheartedly that God is first and last and besides Him there is no other god is certainly impervious to such harm." With due deference to the worthy and pious intention of this writer, the point is that the mere recital of these words has the indicated effect.

In Talmudic times Biblical verses were often employed to heal wounds and diseases, despite rabbinic opposition to this practice. Even stronger was the prohibition against expectorating in the course of such a charm—spitting is a universally recognized magical act, and the authorities sought at least to eliminate this most objectionable feature; it was considered an act of irreverence, they explained, avoiding the true reason.

In later centuries this prohibition was drawn to a fine point, to get around its common transgression. It was limited to those verses in which the name of God occurs, and further "this is forbidden only when the verse is recited after expectorating, for it makes it appear that the name of God has been coupled with that act, and only when the charm is couched in Hebrew. If the name of God is uttered in another tongue, this prohibition does not apply at all." Even the effort to prevent such practices on the Sabbath was unsuccessful. Human need overrode the law, and in cases of serious illness the rabbis consented to be deaf and blind. In such matters law beats futilely against the iron wall of mass will; official Judaism was obliged to bow to popular superstition and accept practices which it would gladly have seen destroyed. These concessions are a tribute to the deep-rooted persistence of superstitious ways of thought and action.

Of all the books which make up the Bible, the Psalms are probably among the most popular verses used in the practice of magic. The book *Shimmush Tehillim*, "The (Magical) Use of the Psalms," opens with the words, "The entire Torah is composed of the names of God, and in consequence it has the property of saving and protecting man." This little work—frequently reprinted in pocket size, and translated into numerous languages—achieved the distinction of being placed on the Index Librorum Prohibitorum of the Catholic Church.

These Psalms are often uttered in faith during the course of casting a spell. Typically, verses are often chosen according to tradition or for a personal interpretation of a certain Psalm. These verses are typically prayed with focused intent and/or conviction. They may be prayed at the altar, over candles, baths, or other objects. In addition, verses may be written on paper and placed under a candle, in a doll, a mojo-bag, or simply carried in one's pocket.

The Bible is also a popular medium used in the practice of Stichomancy, or divination by books, although any book can be used in this practice. Practitioners often have their own systems of operation but generally speaking a question is posed while holding the book, it is then opened to a random page with eyes closed and one's finger is also randomly placed onto a page. The passage on which one's finger falls is then read and interpreted in relation to the question asked.

Divination by the Bible is not limited to simply answering questions in a oracular fashion, in fact, you can use random Bible passages to prescribe rites for your specific issue or condition. The Bible itself contains several instances where magic is performed and spells are prescribed. In the book of Leviticus 16:21-22 , the High Priest ritually passes the sins of the people of Israel onto the head of goat which is then sent out of the city into the desert where it will presumably die taking the sins of the people with it.

A more complex spell occurs in the book of Numbers 15:12-31 a spell is given for a man who believes that his wife has been unfaithful to him that consist, in part, of the Priest gathering dust from the temple and mixing it with holy water. The Priest makes the woman swear an oath that if she has been unfaithful that the water will enter her and become bitter. It will cause her thigh to rot and her belly to swell. The curse is written down and washed away with the water and the woman is made to drink the water. Thereafter if the woman was unfaithful the curse will unfold as described; however, if she was not then no harm will befall her

The process for divining spells out of the Bible is precisely the same as that of divining answers to one's questions as described at the beginning of this article. The only difference here is that certain key words or phrases found in the text will serve as the inspiration for a spell or ritual. For example, let's say that you are interested in starting a romantic relationship with a certain person.

Forbidden Magic Spells From The Bible

You take out your Bible and ask the question "How can I gain (N's) attention and affection?" You open the Bible at random and blindly put your finger on Genesis 1:27 which states: So God created man in his own image, in the image of God created he him; male and female created he them.

It isn't hard for the reader to draw a parallel between the creation of man by God who gathered dust, formed it into a man and breathed life into him and the process of creating a doll-baby and naming it after the person concerned. Therefore, based on this passage alone you may decide to construct a doll baby of both yourself and the object of your affection and ritually bring them together over a number of day, possibly even seven. The ritual could be accompanied by the burning of red-candles and love-drawing incense.

In another instance, let's say that you have a client who comes to you believing that they have been crossed up. They complain that their luck has turned sour, they can't hold on to any money, and their relationships are no longer satisfying. Once again, you go to your Bible and ask "Has (N) been crossed up and if so, how can he find relief?" and this time your finger lands on Psalm 108: 9 which states: Moab is my washpot; over Edom will I cast out my shoe; over Philistia will I triumph.

The words that stand out to me in this verse include "washpot" and "cast out my shoe", which to me is a sign that perhaps someone had thrown for this person by possibly putting down powders that they had walked through. Therefore I would advise the person to burn their shoes and dispose of the ashes at a crossroads. I would also prescribe a foot-washing if not a series of uncrossing baths.

Finally, let's suppose that you have a friend that comes to and says she loves her job, she loves what she does but that her co-worker is just overbearing and is harder on her than other employees. She wants to know what she can do to have a better working relationship with him. You question your Bible and your finger lands on Psalms 104:34, which says: "My meditation on him shall be sweet, I will be glad in the Lord."

In this example, the Bible is practically screaming honey jar! However, based on the word "meditation" and "be glad", I would also recommend that she refrain from having negative thoughts about her co-worker and his or her behavior. Instead I would recommend that she always greet them with a smile, and to simply expect to have only positive encounters with her co-worker.

Forbidden Magic Spells From The Bible

The Bible itself is regarded as a powerful talisman used in many spells and rituals for any number of reasons. The most common use of the Bible as a talisman entails placing one under your head at night so as to prevent nightmares, induce dreams, provide peaceful sleep, or bring prophetic dreams to name a few.

In the days before medical care was accessible to the poor and babies where still delivered by midwives, a Bible was often opened to the book of Matthew (describing the birth of Jesus) and placed on a mother's stomach to ease birth pains and speed up delivery.

Before you enter a new home for the first time, it is said that you should lay an open bible on your doorstep then pick it up and go in your house so that you will be lucky so long as you live in that house. Another source states that a bible in which a dollar has been pressed should be the first thing brought into your new home so that its inhabitants will be righteous and will prosper in all things.

It is believed that spirits will talk to you if you have a bible under your left arm and question it in the name of the Father, Son, and the Holy Ghost.

In some cases, items of special significance such as a four-leaf clover or a child's caul, can be pressed into a bible (either randomly or at a specific verse) to provide good luck to an individual. This presupposes a link between the individual and the item placed in the bible. The belief is such that as the bible preserves the four-leaf clover, for example, so will that individual's luck also be preserved.

Of course these examples pre-suppose that you already have a basic understand of spells, and how to construct them as rarely will a passage simply say something such as "at sunrise light a red candle anointed with Lavender Love Oil and pray Psalm 23 over it nine times...."

The best way to get Bible verses for your own work is simply to read your Bible. When you read a verse or passage that speaks to your spirit, inspires a working, or provides a remedy for a current (or even past) situation then write it down.

187

X. Invoking The Magical Powers of Saints

THE CATHOLIC Church obviously would not call their ritual practices magic. The Church is vehemently opposed to the use of "magic" or witchcraft by laypersons, or those not part of the Church's formal group of clergy. However, the Church's argument against its practice is muddled by contradictions. The Roman Catholic clergy performed regular rituals at worship services where laymen would witness sacraments being performed that invoked God to perform small miracles. The fact that the church could perform "magical" looking rituals on behalf of some people led many to believe that these unendorsed rituals were likewise powerful. Further, the Church could neither stop the use of Christian magic due to its unwillingness to discredit its own practices, nor find a way to discourage its use without admitting the validity of the exercise.

The Roman Catholic Church embraced seven sacraments, many of them potentially magical in nature. The rites of baptism, confirmation, extreme unction, Mass, ordination, penance, and marriage were often considered magical in their application. For instance, during a baptism, a certain ceremony and prayer was performed to exorcise the child of any demonic spirits arising from the sin of conception and childbirth. Another instance of perceived magic took place at a Catholic Mass. One would partake in communion and receive bread and wine, which they believed would transubstantiate into the body and blood of Jesus Christ. According to many Christians during the period of the Reformation, these practices were merely superstitious. That is, the acts and ceremonies were meaningless or were in fact flouting God's law and essential nature. One of Martin Luther's largest contentions was that during Latin ceremonies, the scriptures and acts sounded much like magical incantations.

Forbidden Magic Spells From The Bible

Another facet of Roman Catholic belief was veneration for saints. The church defines a saint as a person who has been particularly holy in life, and after death retains a privileged position in heaven. This tradition allows that Catholics may pray to and ask assistance from those the Catholic Church deemed as saints.

Many Catholics believed that the piety of a saint might be harnessed through use of a talisman. Catholics would carry around amulets or holy "relics" said to be imbued with the spirit and power of a particular saint. This power would be transferred to them through their possession of the blessed scripture or artifact. Individual churches would have patron saints and encourage the worship of a particular saint on his or her specific holy day. For instance, during Medieval times, English villages would often have a representation of Saint Christopher that would "offer a day's preservation from illness or death to all those who looked upon it."

It is believed that any saint, or any Christian for that matter, can pray for any given need on one's behalf. Experience has indicated, however, that certain saints seem to have better results with a particular problem than others. Often this arises out of that saints own trials while on Earth, eg. a saint who was blinded may be helpful for eye problems, a poor saint may empathize with those impoverished, etc. When invoked, a saint may intercede more fervently for problems with which s/he is most familiar.

The use of particular saints for particular problems most likely comes from the ancient Roman religion. When a Roman asked a god or goddess for a certain favor, s/he would cite previous instances, either personal or historical, where that particular favor had been granted by that deity. Also, the public posting of notices granted intercessions arises from Roman custom. So, if you are granted your request through the intercession of a god or saint, do not neglect to make a thanks offering and to acknowledge their help before others.

When asking the Saints to intercede on your behalf, it's most important to be sincere in your petition. Furthermore, it is not wise to ask for that which would be against that particular saint's nature or principals. It is most helpful to think through your request very thoroughly, perhaps even writing it down. Some saints are very appreciative of gifts, sometimes before you make your request, sometimes after and sometimes both.

Forbidden Magic Spells From The Bible

PRAYING FOR AN INTERCESSION

Usually, one's prayers for intercession are accompanied by the burning of candles. Often, simple votive candles are sufficient, but 7 day novena candles of a color appropriate to the saint is even more effective. In addition, some saints have special oils for anointing their candle. Many people also wear the medal of a saint, particularly their patron saint, and carry a prayer card with the picture and prayer to the saint whose intercession is sought.

† The Saints (O.L.= "Our Lady of ...")

St.Anthony Of Padua - Find lost objects, works wonders.

St.Barbara - For love and friendship, conquer enemies.

St.Bernadette - For healing.

Charity, O.L. - Protection of home, find lover, bring prosperity.

St.Christopher - Protection during travel.

St.Dymphna - For mental disorders, demonic possession.

St.Expeditus - Settle disputes, for pressing needs.

Guadelupe, O.L. - Overcome fear, protection from jinxes.

Guardian Angel - Protect self and children from danger and evil spirits.

Forbidden Magic Spells From The Bible

Infant Jesus Of Atocha - Be free from punishment, guilt and sin.

St.Joseph - find job, sell or rent house.

St.Jude - For impossible situations.

St.Lazarus - Healing and Sickness.

St.Martin De Porres - For comfort, health, friends - good life.

St.Martin Caballero - Business, draw customers.

St.Michael - Overcome obstacles, defeat enemes, remove evil.

Mercy, O.L. - Studies, mental clarity

Miraculous Mother - Bring good things of life.

Perpetual Help, O.L. - When in need of help.

St.Peter - Open roads, bring opportunities for success.

St.Ramond - Stop gossip and slander, silence enemies.

St.Raphael - "The Healer of God".

Sacred Heart Of Jesus - Blessed, peaceful life.

Sacred Heart Of Mary - Serenity and spiritual blessings.

Seven African Powers/Saints - All purpose, to solve problems.

NOVENAS

Novenas are a series of devotional prayers, often for special needs and intents. They are generally associated with the number nine, but have also been said in other frequencies, ie. seven. Some novenas, such as to the Infant Jesus of Prague for urgent needs, do require the prayers be said for nine consecutive hours, for nine consecutive days. However done, the use of repetitious devotions over time are said to increase the possibility of obtaining a favorable response to one's petition.

In a traditional novena the devotional candle represents a way to honor a specific saint but it also gives light, energy, and the magic of fire to the devotees' petition or prayer. So it is in our own magic making-we begin with our petition, our intention, or the desire that we wish to manifest. Looking at devotional candles now we often find that when the candles have paper images in the front and prayers in the back there are sometimes lines underneath the prayers for you to write your own petition.

When working with plain devotional candles that do not have any papers or labels affixed to their sides a petition may be written on a small piece of paper and taped to the bottom of the candle or in some cases affixed to the sides of the candle. I have also seen candle shop and botanic owners use a sharpie to inscribe a client's petition directly onto the glass side of the candle. Another popular way to include the petition is to write it into the wax at the top of the candle-using a screwdriver, ice-pick, or blade to inscribe.

If using paper for your petition you may anoint the paper with ritual anointing oil, pass it through ritual incense, anoint it with your own bodily fluids if appropriate, and/or in the case of affixing a piece of paper to the bottom of the candle enclose small bits of personal concerns within the paper, fold, and then tape it to the candle.

Especially popular are Seven Day Novena Candles. These are candles that are encased in glass and are designed to burn for seven consecutive days.

Forbidden Magic Spells From The Bible

When using these candles, each day, for seven days, one is pray before the Novena candle the prayer(s) for that saint and intent. Usually the prayer(s) are printed on the glass container. It is best to say the novena prayer(s) at the same time each day.

Once your candle is ready, it is time to set it. The best practice when working with glass devotional candles is to set them up in a place where they can burn continuously without interruption. A devotional candle should be allowed to sit and burn. You can place them in a large aluminum stock pot, in glass casserole dishes filled with water, sand, or small rocks, in the kitchen sink, in a bathtub, shower, and fire place.

When praying your novena, make the sign of the cross (†) and say "† In the Name of the Father, The Son, and The Hoy Spirit. † Amen.", before and after your novena prayer(s). When your petition is granted be sure to keep any vow that you may have made and to publish a notice of thanksgiving.

† Novena Prayers (To Use With Candles)

St. Clare of Assisi - God of Mercy, You inspired Saint Clare with the love of poverty. By the help of her prayers, may we follow Jesus in His poverty of spirit and come to the joyful vision of Your glory in the Kingdom of Heaven. We ask this through our Lord, Jesus Christ, Your Son, Who lives and reigns with You and the Holy Spirit, One God, forever and ever. Amen.

Blessed Saint Clare, whose very name means light, illumine the darkness of our minds and hearts so we might see what God wishes us to do, and perform it with a willing and joyful heart. Please hear my intentions, Saint Clare.

(Say your intentions here.)

Saint Clare, thank you for hearing me. I know that you will pray for me so I may be made worthy of the promises of Christ. May the Sacred Heart of Jesus be praised, adored, glorified and loved today, and everyday, throughout the world, forever. Amen

St. Barbara - Oh St. Barbara, As your last words to Christ Jesus, before the sword severed your head from your body, were that all those who invoked His Holy Name in memory of you, may find their sins forgotten on the Day of Judgment. Help me in my tribulations; console me in my afflictions and intercede for me and for my family in our needs. Amen (Concentrate on your petition).

St. Expedito - Oh, Glorious Martyr and Protector, St. Expedito! We humbly ask to have fortune and prosperity for our country, that the sick get well, the guilty get pardoned, the just be preserved and those who abandon this valley of tears rest in the Light of The Lord and the souls of the dearly departed rest in peace. † (Mention your request). Amen

Our Lady of Fatima - Most Holy Virgin, who has deigned to come to Fatima to reveal to the three little shepherds the treasures of graces hidden in the recitation of the Rosary, inspire our hearts with a sincere love of this devotion, so that by meditating on the mysteries of our redemption that are recalled in it, we may gather the fruits and obtain the conversion of sinners, and this favor that I so earnestly seek, (say your request here), which I ask of you in this novena, for the greater glory of God, for your own honor, and for the good of all people. Amen

St. Jude - Most Holy Apostle, St. Jude, Faithful Servant And Friend Of Jesus, pray for me who am so despaired in this hour of great need. Bring visible and speedy help for I promise you, O Blessed St. Jude to be ever mindful of this great favor. I will never cease to honor you as my most special, most powerful patron. Amen.

St. Lazarus - Oh Blessed Saint Lazarus, Patron of the Poor, I believe in you and call on your most holy spirit to grant me my favor. † In The Name Of The Father, The Son, and The Holy Spirit. I trust in your infinite goodness to intercede for me through Jesus Christ, Our Lord to grant me this petition (mention petition). Amen

St. Martha - I resort to thy aid and protection. As proof of my affection and faith, I offer thee this light, which I shall burn every Tuesday. Comfort me in all my difficulties and through the great favors thou didst enjoy when the Savior was lodged in thy house, intercede for my family that we be provided for in our necessities. I ask of thee, Saint Martha, to overcome all difficulties as thou didst overcome the dragon which thou hadst at thy feet. In the name of the Father and of the Son and of the Holy Spirit. Amen

Miraculous Mother - Oh, Miraculous Mother! With inspired confidence I call upon thee to extend thy merciful, loving kindness so that thy powers of perpetual help will protect me and assist me in my needs and difficulties. Please grant me my desire. Amen (Mention petition).

St. Michael - Oh Glorious Archangel St. Michael, watch over me during all my life. Defend me against the assaults of the demon. Assist me, especially at the hour of my death. Obtain for a favorable judgment and help me in all my needs. Amen.

O.L.-Perpetual Help - Oh Mother of Perpetual Help, grant that I may ever invoke thy most powerful name. O purest Mary, O sweetest Mary, let thy name henceforth be ever on my lips. Delay not, O Blessed Lady, to help me whenever I call on thee. For in all my needs, in all my temptations, I shall never cease to call on thee, ever repeating thy sacred name, Mary, Mary. I will not be content with merely pronouncing thy name, but let my love for thee prompt me ever to hail thee, Mother Of Perpetual Help. Amen

St. Rita of Cascia - O Holy Patroness of those in need, St. Rita, whose pleadings before thy Divine Lord are almost irresistible, who for thy lavishness in granting favors hast been called the Advocate of the hopeless and even of the impossible; St. Rita, so humble, so pure, so mortified, so patient and of such compassionate love for thy Crucified Jesus that thou couldst obtain from Him whatsoever thou askest, on account of which all confidently have recourse to thee expecting, if not always relief, at least comfort; be propitious to our petition, showing thy power with God on behalf of thy suppliant; be lavish to us, as thou hast been in so many wonderful cases, for the greater glory of God, for the spreading of thine own devotion, and for the consolation of those who trust in thee. We promise, if our petition is granted, to glorify thee by making known thy favor, to bless and sing thy praises forever. Relying then upon thy merits and power before the Sacred Heart of Jesus, we pray thee grant that (here mention your request).

Pray for us, O holy Saint Rita, that we may be made worthy of the promises of Christ. Amen

Seven African Powers - Oh, Seven African Powers, who so close to Our Divine Savior, with great humility I kneel before you and implore your intercession before The Almighty. Hear my petition that I may glory in your powers to protect me, to help me and provide for my needs. Amen

St. Thérèse - O Little Thérèse of the Child Jesus, please pick for me a rose from the heavenly gardens and send it to me as a message of love. O Little Flower of Jesus, ask God today to grant the favors I now place with confidence in your hands...

(Make your request here...)

St. Thérèse, help me to always believe as you did, in God's great love for me, so that I might imitate your "Little Way" each day. Amen

HOW TO INTERPRET YOUR CANDLE

After you have completed your prayer, there are several ways to read your candle to check whether or not your plea of intercession was heard. Just like reading tea leaves, the burnt candles can provide valuable insight.

For example: If the Candle explodes, this means that the candle caught something negative that was being directed towards you or your home, especially if the candle is for protective purposes. If you are using the candle to dominate or to influence someone, then that person has very strong spiritual protection.

If for some reason your candle will not stay lit: If you are burning for protection, then you had better do some spiritual cleansing before this candle can be of service.

Candle Flame significance: High Flame – spell is going to work good and work fast. Low flame – spell will take longer, and probably more work or a different method needed in order to be successful.

Forbidden Magic Spells From The Bible

The soot on a candle is one of the most recognizable results of burning a candle. While in the mundane world one might say this was merely soot, in the spiritual we know there is a message to be interpreted in that soot.

Black soot is a sign of negativity and witchcraft. If the soot does not travel all the way down the glass, is only at the top or perhaps stops in the middle, the negative influence or obstacle has been unblocked. If the black goes down the entire length of the candle it means your working has been blocked and there are still things preventing you for attaining your desired result. It could also indicate someone has casted against you or has significant spiritual protection. If this is the case burn another candle to try to break through their defenses.

If the soot is at the bottom of the candle it is a warning that negative influences are being sent to you. This can be the case when someone casts against you.

White soot can indicate spiritual communication, purity, and exorcism. It could indicate that the spirits have heard your prayers and removed the negativity from the working. This is especially true in unhexing rituals, but you need to look to the amount of soot to tell you if it is completed or not.

If the soot only goes half way down or less, the intercession was successful. If the soot is carried through the length of the candle you may need further cleansing and spiritual work.

If the soot is at the bottom of the candle, it signifies the presence of outside aid or help either spiritually or physically.

If the candle burned half black and half white this means that one aspect is overriding the other. Look to which is on top to see what was undone. If black is on top, your spirits cleared it. If white is on top the spirits of another have combated your attempts.

If the soot is on only one side of the candle, this is a sign that what you are doing is incorrect. Either the candle fixing wasn't appropriate or the petitioned Saints/Angels are not happy with the candle itself.

The glass retains the story of the working through the soot and preparation but the glass itself can tell you things about the spell. If the glass cracks but does not break it means there was some type of opposition that was broken. It may have been sent to the spell to try to deflect it or it may have been encountered along the way. If it does not break or shatter then the spell is protected and was successfully defended.

If the glass breaks or shatters it means you are up against something larger than yourself. Malicious forces have either protected your target or have been attracted to your working and are trying to interfere. It can also indicate someone is casting against you and you are not spiritually protected or strong enough as what was thrown at you was larger than what you were sending out. Either way, do a stronger working and light another candle to try to combat it.

The flame is by far the most important part of any candle working. The subtle actions of the flame can tell you a lot from the moment you light it, to the moment it goes out. If the candle does not light this means that this type of working will not work for what you need and another type of spell should be used.

If the candle lights and splits into two or more flames, this indicates the presence of others, either spirits, deities, or human, getting involved. Look to the rest of the candle to interpret whether this person is good or bad.

If you are trying to split up a couple and both flames stay lit, the couple will stay together.

If you are doing a working for attract a lover and the second flame seems to rise out of the wax your working will be successful especially if both flames grow into one large flame.

If the candle flame is high it means there is a lot of power behind the spell and little resistance. If the candle burns low it means there is a strong opposing spiritual force and a cleansing and or banishing may be needed.

If the flame makes a crackling or popping sound it indicates conversation. Either the spirits are trying to talk to you or the target is talking about you. Look to the purpose of the candle and the other actions of the flame to determine which is which.

If the flame flickers there is a spirit around. If the flame pops while flickering, it is the spirit trying to communicate to you. Open yourself up to it. If it is a devotional candle and it is flickering it means you are in contact with your deity and any prayers or petitions will be heard.

If you attempt to blow out the flame and it does not go out this means the spirit does not want you to extinguish it. The same can be said if you blow it out and it flicks back on. Let the spirit complete its work, something important may be in the works that you do not want to interrupt. If you are uncomfortable ask the spirit to protect the candle or ask for permission and try to extinguish it again.

If the entire top of the prepared candle catches fire it means all the resources of the prepared candle are being used due to spiritual influences creating obstacles. Look to the other signs to see if the candle was successful. If the preparations do not collect along the glass as the candle burns, but remain pooled together, it means all the resources are needed and will burn at the end of the candle. The soot, flame, and glass should be read for the outcome.

If the flame burns high and calm and produces no soot you are in the presence of a larger entity or guardian spirit, most likely benevolent. The same can be said for high aggressive flames that flicker in large strokes. These tend to be darker spirits and deities, both are there to listen or aid you.

If the flame goes out while burning this means the spirits cannot help you and the answer you seek is already determined. This can also happen if you unexpectedly get the result before the candle is finished.